GW00854072

Drama Toolkit

Sketches and guidelines for exploring the Bible through drama

by GORDON and RONNI LAMONT

A Bible Society Creative Handbook

For churches, teachers, and drama group leaders

BIBLE SOCIETY

Stonehill Green, Westlea, Swindon SN5 7DG, England

All material © Gordon & Ronni Lamont 1989, except:

Peck at Paradise	© Kevin Daniel 1989
Jonah and *Kenan & Son*	© Stephen Deal 1989
St Sharon's and *The Baker*	© Nick Page 1989
Rubble Blues	© Frank McGregor 1989
The Beatitudes	© Richard & Sue Cooper 1989
No Room	© Derek Haylock 1989

All rights reserved. No part of this publication may be reproduced, stored in a retrieval system, or transmitted, in any form or by any means, electronic, mechanical, photocopying or otherwise without the prior permission of The British and Foreign Bible Society.

Unless otherwise stated, quotations from the Bible are from the Good News Bible, published by the Bible Societies/Collins, © American Bible Society, New York, 1966, 1971, 1976.

Quotations from the Bible in *The Beatitudes* are from the New International Version, published by Hodder & Stoughton Limited, © New York International Bible Society, 1978.

First published 1989

British Library Cataloguing in Publication Data

Lamont, Gordon
Drama Toolkit.
1. Christian church. Parish life. Group activities.
Drama use of Bible
I. Title   II. Lamont, Ronni
259'.8

ISBN 0-564-05415-1

Important: Please read

The dramatic material in this book may be performed free of charge, providing that the following conditions are met:

1. That the performance is by an amateur group

2. For performance before a live non-paying audience

3. That the authors of the work performed are properly credited in any programme or hand-out

4. The above does not confirm any right to perform any of the material in the book on television, radio, film, video or audio recording, or in any other way except as stated above.

For performances that do not fall within these conditions, you are requested to contact Bible Society, at the address above, to make appropriate arrangements.

Please note

The permission granted above applies only in respect of performances. No part of this book may be copied without specific permission from the publisher. It therefore follows that unless you have obtained such permission (for which a charge may be made), you should purchase sufficient copies of the book to enable you to rehearse any dramatic piece from it.

Bible Societies exist to provide resources for Bible distribution and use. Bible Society in England and Wales (BFBS) is a member of the United Bible Societies, an international partnership working in over 180 countries. Their common aim is to reach all people with the Bible, or some part of it, in a language they can understand and at a price they can afford. Parts of the Bible have now been translated into approximately 1,800 languages. Bible Societies aim to help every church at every point where it uses the Bible. You are invited to share in this work by your prayers and gifts. The Bible Society in your country will be very happy to provide details of its activity.

Contents

Foreword

When I was in the third year at school, rejoicing over being the first in my class to wear a pair of flares, the word "workshop" meant Monday afternoons, double Design and Tech, up to my elbows in sawdust. Now, however, I've swapped bench for stage, flares for jogging trousers, and my toolkit has become a shelf of drama books (well, almost).

This book is a welcome addition. It has a lot for anyone who is into constructing their own drama, joining a drama group, or extending their knowledge of working on texts and other practical books on the performing arts, and Gordon and Ronni have a proven record of being able to take people with an interest in drama, and inspiring them to produce and perform great things.

PHILIP HAWTHORN

Prelude

Creating drama

We'd like to admit our bias from the start. Drama is important to us. It's part of our lives, part of our worship, and part of our understanding of God. We have a love for, and a commitment to, drama and dance in Church life. Why?

If you read some books or hear certain Christians talk, they can be very clear on why we and others like us have this commitment to drama: it's part of our fallen nature, something to do with a desire for self-glorification, for fame, success, and the love of applause. They see drama as something alien to the life of a Christian, or at least peripheral – OK for a bit of entertainment but with as much connection to worship as a copy of *The Beano!*

Our answer to this is to talk about what drama means to us, and how it helps us to worship God and understand him – in other words how drama is central to our lives as Christians.

We are all dramatic

Claire is nineteen months old as we write. She can only say a few words – "sock" being her clearest and favourite, with "shoe" a close second (maybe she'll grow up to write a "Footwear Toolkit"). One of her favourite games is for Gordon to chase her on all fours. She runs away shrieking, and when he catches and tickles her she has a wonderful giggle. She likes to be caught and she likes to run away. She pretends to be frightened but she knows it's only a game. She is playing "as if". Everyone plays "as if" at some time or another.

You may be going to speak to a group of people, perhaps in a sermon or at a youth group, so you prepare what you're going to say. Do you also practise it (in your mind or out loud), "as if" it were happening now?

You are going for an interview for a job. Do you think about what you'll be asked? Does the whole thing turn into a little drama in your mind? Do you picture the room, the people, the first question? In other words, do you place yourself, in your imagination, "as if" you were being interviewed now?

You are in first-century Palestine. You are listening to a man telling a story about a farmer with two sons. One son takes his inheritance and goes. Is this a boring academic story or do you use your powers of imagination to feel the story "as if" it were happening to you? Do you understand the story because you can step, for a moment, out of your present reality (sitting, listening) into the reality of the story?

Drama is all about "as if" and to be dramatic in this sense is the most natural thing in the world. God has made us that way.

Creating drama

This book takes "as if" a stage further. To move from "as if" to drama, you need take only one simple step – move into the "as if" world with someone else.

You're preparing for that interview. Instead of just thinking what will happen, you get a friend to ask you some questions "as if" they were the interviewer and you answer "as if" you are being interviewed now. Two people entering the world of "as if" create drama. You don't need a separate audience because you are both the audience and the participants.

When Jesus told a story there was an audience of listeners. He and his listeners entered the "as if" world together, and together they created drama in the form of dramatic story telling.

Suppose you want to explore with a church congregation the implications of the good Samaritan story. You could present a sketch, *Traveller Casserole*, which you can find on page 48 of this book. The congregation enter into the situation and are enabled to explore it because of the power of "as if" – the power of drama!

Drama and us

We use drama quite naturally as a way of helping us to make sense of our lives, of understanding God and his world. This is not some trendy add-on to our Christianity, it is right there at the heart of our faith. We follow the example of Jesus who opened up difficult questions about God and his kingdom by inviting his hearers into an "as if" world:

■ "as if" the kingdom of God is a tree

■ "as if" faith is a grain of mustard seed

■ "as if" the world is a field

- "as if" Jesus is a sower

In this book we provide tried and tested ways into the "as if" world, using drama to explore the depth and richness of the Christian faith.

When we first performed at the Greenbelt Festival, we remember most clearly a poster in the dressing room that read, "The Son of Man came to serve, not to be served". This seemed completely right in the context of a Christian theatre event. Drama is not about self-glorification but should be used as one of God's good gifts for exploring and understanding his world.

Use drama to serve, in aiding understanding, and in helping people to enter fully into God's Kingdom.

How to use this book

This is not simply another book of religious drama and dance material. There is good material from a wide range of Christian writers and performers, but each piece is linked with ideas and suggestions for getting the most out of it and for creating your own work using similar styles and approaches. *Drama Toolkit* contains two kinds of material, "Frameworks" and "Presentations".

The frameworks give ideas for the creation of drama, usually with suggestions for how to approach a Bible passage and explore it using the drama strategies under discussion. Each framework (except "Games and Exercises") is followed by several presentations.

Presentations are sketches and movement pieces from ourselves and other authors.

Like any toolkit, the idea is that you take what you need, when you need it. A less experienced group might like to work through each framework, trying out the presentations that follow, before choosing one piece to work on in more depth. Another group may completely ignore the presentations but use one or more of the frameworks to build on and develop their own material.

Use the book in the way that suits your group and its needs. It is probably a good idea if someone from the group reads the whole book first, so you have an idea of the sort of tools offered. We very much hope that after this, *Drama Toolkit* will become a valuable "ideas generator", a source of inspiration for *your own* work.

GORDON AND RONNI LAMONT

Here is a diagram showing areas of the stage which are referred to throughout the book.

upstage right	upstage centre	upstage left
Centre stage right	centre stage	centre stage left
downstage right	downstage centre	downstage left

AUDIENCE

Your attention is drawn to the copyright notice on page ii.

1. Frameworks and presentations

Introduction

"Frameworks" are concerned with ways of creating drama. We give practical suggestions for the development of ideas, situations, and characters, and ways to put these "on their feet". The result can be drama and theatre of depth and interest, well structured and effective.

A framework is something to build upon. It isn't the building and it isn't the builder. The building is the finished piece of theatre in its entirety with the audience and what they take from it. The builders are those who create the work – you!

You must use the frameworks in the way that seems best to you, so don't be afraid to play around and have some fun with the ideas in this book. One useful way of working might be for your group to set aside some time to explore these ways of working and others which group members may know of. Do this without the pressure of building towards a performance or presentation of any kind. This will have the effect of helping you explore new ideas together in a relaxed manner, and will probably do a lot for your group identity. A colleague of ours describes this as "working glue".

Another way of using these ideas is to relate them to specific scripts such as the ones in this book. The pieces which follow each framework are provided to give examples of dramatic material which could be developed using the ideas just explored. However, no framework can really be seen as a "watertight compartment", so ideas from other sections may also be appropriate. For this reason, our choice of which pieces follow which framework may not be yours. The golden rule is if you have an idea, try it!

Working with a writer

The ideas in the frameworks can be used by a group to create a piece of theatre for themselves, but this should not rule out the possibility of working with a writer or writers, or with an existing script. The writer may be involved in workshops with the group, exploring the themes and issues of the piece of work to be created. They may present ideas or a first draft for the group to explore using various frameworks, and the group would then report back to the writer with the results of their research.

Using the ideas in this book should not in any sense diminish the role of a writer, but should enhance the working relationship between writer and group and the group's understanding of the writer's work.

Working with a director

It is perfectly possible to create a piece of theatre without the use of a director but we are assuming that in most instances, when using the techniques and strategies in this book, your group will be working with someone leading the session. The precise role of this person will vary from group to group and with individual working styles. It is our view that the best directors work in a collaborative fashion with their group and see their functions as supportive.

Essentially, a director provides an "outside eye", and is able to look at the group's work from a different perspective. The director will provide an opportunity for all members of the group to suggest a way forward when working on an improvisation or text, but we would also expect the working company to respect the director's unique position of outside eye.

As in all matters dramatic, each individual and group must find their own working arrangements and pattern, and if you are used to working together this may not be a problem. However, it might be good to use the opportunity of working from this book to try different working styles, perhaps encouraging different members of the group to take on a directorial role in running workshops and later in working on presentations.

The role of the director

If the role of workshop leader/director is new to you, may we offer the following as possible working guidelines.

1. Fill the gap

The "gap" is what happens at the beginning of your workshop session. You know the sort of thing – everyone looks at everyone else until someone tentatively offers a starting point. This kind of uncertainty should be avoided, particularly if people are new to each other and feeling a little unsure about what they've let themselves in for. The director should have some sort of working framework for the session and a clear starting point. Plan flexibility so that you can take ideas and suggestions from the group, but still have enough to keep things going – fill the gap!

2. Have an aim

Know what you're doing and why. If that seems a bit of a tall order then at least try to work out a general direction for your work together in a session. You might aim simply to go for "working glue" (see page 1), or you might want to explore the notion of building characters, or understanding more about dramatic tension. In a sense, the aim can be anything just so long as you have one that can act as a motor for the whole session and keep things moving.

3. Be supportive

Your group wants things to happen, they want to get somewhere, to achieve something. We all respond better to positive than to negative comments. Use this. You don't have to pretend that something works if it doesn't, and you shouldn't have to lower your artistic standards just to keep people happy. Your supportiveness exists in doing your bit to create a positive attitude within the group.

Try to create the time to try things out, and let the actors know that the work belongs to them as much as you. After all, once a piece of theatre is in performance the actors will have far more say in what is happening than the director will! It's very difficult to give advice on being supportive. In essence, it all comes back to the leader seeing themselves as one member of the group with a specific function to perform which is intended to be for the benefit of all involved, rather than as someone with all the answers.

2. Games and exercises

In this framework we aim to give you some ideas for games and exercises to use at your group sessions, together with some suggestions for when and why to use them. The list is far from exhaustive; you'll have your own favourite games and you can get plenty of other games and exercises from the books listed in our bibliography at the back of this book.

Games

Getting together

The following games are good for bringing the group together by creating some fun at the start of your session.

Names

The leader gives the group one minute to go around shaking hands with each person, giving their name as they do so. After this, the game is repeated with individuals changing names as they shake. So Meredith shakes hands with Cathy – the next time he shakes hands, instead of offering his name as Meredith, he calls himself Cathy. This time he shakes hands with Tim so Tim becomes Cathy and Meredith (who was Cathy) is now Tim . . . and so on. The whole group are doing this at once. A refinement is to ask people to sit out when they are unable to remember who they are supposed to be!

Instant animals

The group leader calls out a number and the group have to get into groups of that number. So, you call out "four" and instantly there are groups of four. Any who are not in such a group simply stay in for the next go when you call out another number. Once you've got this going, get the group to try it in absolute silence for a few goes and then add this refinement. After you've called the number, give the name of an animal. Each group has to form itself into a picture of that animal – without talking! Any who are not in a group of the right size must make the animal and an appropriate noise until you call out the next number and animal.

Still images

These games will fit well with the ideas in the Still images framework (see page 42), and your group will work in smaller groups (3, 4, or 5 people) for these two games.

Titles

Give each group a title and explain that you want them to make a still picture representing that title. Some examples are:

- A Day at the Races
- Monkey Business
- A Night at the Opera
- At the Circus
- Go West
- The Big Store

- *The Classroom*
- *The Football Match*
-

When the groups have worked these out, making them as comic as they can, take just a short time to look at and enjoy each other's pictures.

Before and after

Next, go on to "before and after" pictures (i.e. two still pictures that tell a story of some dramatic event, missing out the actual event). Each group chooses their own situation and prepares the two pictures without letting the others hear what it's all about. After five to ten minutes the groups share their pictures and everyone else has to try to guess what happened in between.

Following bodies

Select a leader who sets off moving about the room. The next person chooses part of the leader's body and follows that, always keeping their head the same distance from the chosen bit of body. So, Heather leads, John chooses to follow Heather's elbow, moving about the room keeping six inches from it at all times. This will involve John in a fair bit of ducking and weaving. Wendy follows John's ankle and Paul follows Wendy's knee (and so on – try it for a good laugh).

Salad

You need chairs for this one – one chair for each member of the group, minus one. The chairs are placed in a circle. The leader has no chair and from the centre of the circle gives each group member the name of part of a salad. Go round naming, cucumber, lettuce, tomato, and onion, until everyone is named one of four bits of salad.

The leader has no seat and so calls out one of the bits of salad. Everyone in that category must get up and swop places with someone else from that group. At the same time, the leader is looking for a seat, which may mean that a new person is in the middle at the start of the next round. This new person calls out cucumber, lettuce, tomato, or onion, and the game continues. If the person in the middle calls "salad", then everyone must get up and find a new seat.

Building concentration

These games serve a similar function to those in "Getting Together", but they put more of an emphasis on group focus and concentration.

Grandmother's footsteps

An old favourite, but just in case you don't know it, a group member stands facing a wall. The rest of the group start from an opposite wall and have to creep up and touch "Grandmother" on the shoulder. "Grandmother" may turn around at any point, and if she sees anyone move they are sent back to the start. A variation on this is to put "Grandmother" in the centre of the room and place everyone else around her in a big circle. "Grandmother" must constantly turn around to see if people are moving and while her back is turned . . . If you've not tried this variation of a well-known game, you'll find it adds an interesting new dimension.

Hissing Sid

This is best in a fairly enclosed space. Everyone except the leader closes their eyes or, better still, is blindfolded. The leader taps someone on the shoulder to be the snake, who also remains blindfolded. The game begins. Everyone must keep moving at all times. The snake has to listen for where people are, move up to them and "kill" them by gripping their arm and making a short hissing noise. The rest of the group try to listen for the snake and keep out of its way. If killed, a participant removes the blindfold and retires to the edge to watch. This game gets very tense and, quite apart from anything else, will make the group appreciate the power of silence!

Invisible clay

This is a game for pairs. The partners find a space and sit facing each other a couple of feet apart. One partner picks up an invisible lump of clay and decides to make something out of it. They begin to shape the clay as appropriate. Imagining the clay to be real, they work, shape, and knead it toward the finished object. The partners are not allowed to communicate, A simply watches B as B works. The group leader calls "Change" and A takes over B's work, continuing to make the same object. Change again, and perhaps again.

The leader then stops the game and the participants say what they think they were making. A variation is to play the game with the whole group in a circle passing the object around. This is best after you've played the other version a few times on different occasions.

Drama toolkit

This can be played with any two words – even nonsense words (which of course cannot be applied to *Drama Toolkit*!). The group sits or stands in a circle, and the leader passes "drama" around, by looking to the person next to them (left or right) and saying "drama". This is simply passed around the circle by people saying "drama" to the person next to them. The only other rule is that you change direction by saying "toolkit". You say "drama" when passing in the same direction (either left or right, depending on which direction it came to you) and "toolkit" when you want to change direction. This is one of those games that sounds totally daft on paper and seems simple once you get the hang of it, but actually requires good concentration to play for any length of time.

Exercises

This section contains suggestions for some simple exercises to help loosen up bodies ready for the session to come. Use a selection of these, or better still, work with someone who can lead a good work out/warm up. For more exercise ideas see our book *Move Yourselves*.

Working it out

If your group has only just started working together we recommend one of these for every session, but please take note of the physical abilities of your group as exercise needs to be handled carefully. It might be a good idea to get someone with experience to lead the group in exercise sessions.

1. Loose

Standing up, place your right hand in front of you. Shake the hand, trying to keep the movement isolated in the hand. Then let the shake travel up the wrist, then the elbow, the shoulder, and so on. Once the whole arm is going, bring in the other hand . . . the wrist, etc.

When both arms are moving, start off with a foot, keeping the top half on the go, then the other leg, etc. This should end up with people jumping all over the place and really letting go of their inhibitions. You may like to use some music once folk are off the spot.

2. Tense

This is a repeat of the above, but instead of shaking the movement is painfully tense and controlled.

3. Shake out

Everyone, standing up, has their arms downwards, and backs arched, like puppets with cut strings. Put on some music with a hefty beat and as the music comes in, slowly start to move from the fingers first, then wrists, elbows, etc., until everyone is leaping all over the place. Appoint a leader for the group to follow if they start to flag. Then let everyone flop on to the floor and relax for a few moments – they'll need it.

The object of the following exercises is to prevent you cricking your necks or dislocating various parts of the anatomy that you would prefer to stay joined together when you start work seriously.

These exercises are more specifically targeted at different parts of the body.

Body rollers

Shoulders

We like to start these with the shoulders. Get the group to consciously register where their shoulders lie. Now pick them up, so they are up round your ears, and replace them as far back as you can. Now repeat, but replace them as far forward as possible. Work through this several times, middle, back, forward, etc., speeding up as you go along.

Follow this with a short burst of lifting and lowering, first both shoulders together, then one up, one down, and so on. Tension tends to concentrate in the shoulders, so do work at these exercises.

Head

Now slowly do some head rolls, first one way, then the other.

Ater that, drop your head into your chest, then flop it as far back as you can, letting your jaw gape open – your head goes back further like that! Repeat several times, then drop your head to the left and then to the right a few times, looking forward all the time. Finish this off by turning your head to look to the left and then to the right several times.

Arms

Having done your shoulders and neck, finish them off by throwing your arms backwards in a circular motion a few times, then forwards a few times. Finish off by giving your arms a good shake.

Torso

To bring your torso into life, do some side bends, making sure that you keep your back upright, as if you were sandwiched between two sheets of glass, one behind and one in front.

Follow this by stretching. Reach up above your heads using alternate arms eight times. Then bend from the small of the back to a "flat back" and reach forward from this flat back eight times. Then, keeping knees straight, touch your toes eight times, then repeat the flat-back stretch. It is important for you to realize that it is very difficult to flat back at 90 degress to your legs without a lot of practice. When you start, don't expect to get very far!

9

Finishing off

Fast exercises

To really finish yourselves off, slap your hip bones with your hands and then stretch up, slap hips (front!) and touch toes and repeat, quickly, lots of times. You'll find that the floor gets closer very rapidly. As an alternative to slap up, slap down, put your hands on your hips, and push your elbows back (like a chicken). Then stretch down one leg to grab your ankle with both hands for two pulls, replace your hands on your hips and "chicken" again, to go down to the other ankle.

If you're feeling really keen, you can put on some good music and go through the whole lot two or three times.

Relaxing the tension away

Many people are now familiar with relaxation techniques, be it from attending ante-natal courses or whatever. For those of you who don't have that experience, here's how to do it – or at least, one way. It's easiest lying down. Most people choose to lie on their backs, but lying on one's side or stomach ("foetal" or "recovery" positions) can be easier. If you are on your back, make sure that your head is looking slightly higher than you would if you were in bed, or to one side.

Now concentrate on your hands. Pull them up into fists, clenching them tightly, then let them relax. Do this a couple of times, then think your way up first one arm, then the other, tensing and relaxing the muscles. Spend quite a long time in your shoulders, then start the whole process off at your feet. Work up your body, then do your neck and head. It is very hard to relax your neck muscles – it's not something we do unless almost asleep. Practise this until you can do it really quickly – it can work wonders for the blood pressure.

Relaxed concentration

While the group are in this semi-soporific state, try out a few exercises for concentration.

As quietly as you can, walk around the space and then make a noise. Click your fingers or tap two pencils, and see if everyone, with eyes closed, can point to the source of the noise. Repeat this a few times, and then get them to count how many noises they can isolate from outside of the room, from inside the room, or from inside their body. Discuss this afterwards and see how incredibly alert you can be while physically being very relaxed.

3. Character framework

The situation

◼ Two members of your group are to perform a sketch based on the parable of the widow and the judge (from Luke, chapter 18). The rest of the group will be working with them as they explore and develop characterizations. You're the director.

Scene one

◼ The session starts at 7.30 pm. It's now 8.10 and you're about to begin. You start by calling everyone to order. You continue to call people to order. You call everyone to order and the session starts at 8.15. (except for Jim and Meredith who arrive at 8.20 and start at 8.35 with a cup of coffee and a chat).

Scene two

◼ You ask for ideas as to how Molly should play the part of the widow. Bob says she should play her as a woman who's lost her husband. This is followed by discussion. Sue says the widow should have only one leg as an outward symbol of her loss. James quotes Leviticus and there is a respectful silence – followed by a stunned silence. This is followed up by a period of silence.

Scene three

◼ Meredith suggests the group do a sketch by Riding Lights. This is unanimously agreed. Perhaps you should do the same one as you did last month – this too is agreed, and the director is thanked for her innovative working practices. Jim proposes a cup of coffee. Cathy wonders if group finances extend to a trip to the pub. James quotes Leviticus and coffee is served.

If you've turned to this framework looking for help when working with the sort of characters quoted above with their idiosyncratic ideas and approaches to punctuality – sorry! This framework is all about creating dramatic characters, not dealing with real-life ones (although the above group sound quite keen and lively compared with some!).

What we hope we can offer are some ideas to help fill some of those silences. Characters are, of course, of the utmost importance in a piece of theatre and in this framework we aim to give some suggestions for strategies that your group can use to help them move from, "I play the part of the good Samaritan's donkey" to, "I am the good Samaritan's donkey, and this is the sort of donkey I am!"

As in other frameworks, we'll give a practical example to aid our understanding of the various working strategies. We'll use a Bible passage but all of these ways of working can be used when developing characters, while rehearsing a script, or when devising drama from other source material. We've chosen a simple two-character parable from Luke's Gospel.

The parable of the widow and the judge

Then Jesus told his disciples a parable to teach them that they should always pray and never become discouraged. "In a certain town there was a judge who neither feared God nor respected man. And there was a widow in that same town who kept coming to him and pleading for her rights, saying, 'Help me against my opponent!' For a long time the judge refused to act, but at last he said to himself, 'Even though I don't fear God or respect man, yet because of all the trouble this widow is giving me, I will see to it that she gets her rights. If I don't, she will keep on coming and finally wear me out!'"

(Luke 18.1–5)

Lists and notes

We find it most useful when working on characters to stick some big sheets of paper on the wall on which we can record ideas and thoughts as the session progresses. This has two valuable uses; as well as keeping a record of ideas, individuals can jot down thoughts that occur during the session which might break someone else's flow of thought if they were voiced immediately.

Start by making lists of what you know from the story about the two characters in it. We know that really we have three characters mentioned here if we include the story-teller in verse 1, but for now just use the characters from within the story. Your lists might end up something like this:

Widow	Judge
■ Seeks justice	■ Doesn't fear God
■ Needs help	■ Doesn't fear man
■ Is persistent	■ Lives in the town
■ Knows the judge	■ Gives in to constant demands
■ Has an opponent	■ Can be practical when it suits him
■ Lives in the town	■ Knows the widow

Already, from such a short story, you have a lot to be going on with. Let's focus, for now, on just one of the characters – the judge.

We'll assume that you have your sheets up and have recorded on the judge's sheet the above characteristics. You're now ready to explore and develop the character using the following strategies.

Tell a story

Take one of the characteristics; for example, "Doesn't fear man". You are now going to tell a story that illustrates this characteristic. You can do this in pairs or a larger group. Each person tells a sentence of the story before passing on to the next. The idea is to develop the story not to block each other's ideas. Try creating a story about the judge standing up to tough guys, or dealing with the tax collector. The important thing is to have some fun with this. Don't worry if the story doesn't seem very likely or realistic as, very often, a quite unlikely story can be used to suggest more realistic characteristics.

What you will be doing by using this process is "fleshing out" the character's background. For example, we know that the judge doesn't fear man but perhaps your story will demonstrate this quality linked with a sense of humour or with terrible arrogance or disregard for his own safety. After you've done a few quick stories, choose those that you want to use in the character's background, jot down the essential points on your large sheets of paper (for reference throughout the session) and then move into hot-seating.

Hot-seating

The basic strategy involves the rest of the group asking questions of the actor playing the character in question. This is a natural development from *Tell a story* above. We're going to look at a number of strategies that can be grouped under the general heading of hot-seating.

Hot-seating – *character under pressure*

This is the most basic form of hot-seating. An actor takes the chair and is addressed as the character they are playing. The rest of the group ask questions of the character. Any question that the character may be expected to know about or be able to express an opinion on is permissible. The rest of the group pile on the questions without allowing time for reflection or "making up an answer".

Pros

- Helps the actor get into the full details of the character's life.
- Can give confidence to the playing of the character – "I really do know this character, I can think with their mind".
- It's quick to use and helps move your session along.

Cons

- Is probably best used when the character is well researched already or if the actor is particularly at home with this kind of fast, "think on your feet" improvisation.
- Can lead to actors giving the obvious immediate reaction rather than a well thought out, less stereotypical response.

Hot-seating – *many actors, one character*

If your group or individuals within it are nervous or uncertain about the skills needed for *Character under pressure*, then this strategy uses a similar technique but offers greater protection to the individual.

To explore the character of the judge, invite three people to take on the role of the judge while the rest of the group asks them questions as if speaking to the judge. This takes the pressure off one individual and allows the process to be shared within the group.

Pros

- Shares the task more equally within the group.
- Allows for a wider range of responses.

Cons

- Requires considerable sensitivity not to talk over each other or contradict one another.

Hot-seating – symbol as character

Ask the group to choose an object to represent the character. Give time for the group to make suggestions and, if this is practical, to search out the chosen object. Next, place the object on the chair or in a position of focus and have the group concentrate on that while asking questions. One person can answer for the character or several as in *Many actors, one character* above, but the point is that the actor is not the focus, the object is.

To explore the character of the judge in this way, you could place a coat as if it were a robe of office, or a book to represent the Law, or simply turn the chair with its back to the group to represent his lack of concern.

You could place several objects and turn this into a valuable exercise in itself; "What would we choose to represent the judge? What do these objects tell us about his character?"

Pros

■ Perhaps a more thoughtful method than other hot-seating strategies. Good for a thoughtful group who are not happy to move directly into more "dramatic" activities.
■ Protects the actor(s) answering the questions by making the object(s) the specific focus of the group.

Cons

■ Can get bogged down in intellectualizing rather than developing character.

Hot-seating – endowment

Endowment is a kind of hot-seating in reverse. The actor sits in the hot seat and the rest of the group endow him or her with various characteristics. The group might, in endowing the character of the judge, say things like, "You're forty years old"; "All you really want to do is retire", or "You've been getting half a stone heavier every year for the past ten years". The actor simply listens and mentally notes these characteristics. They may take them on as they listen (sitting differently when weight is mentioned, for example). Endowment can then lead on to any of the hot-seating strategies as above.

Pros

■ This is a two-way process to which the whole group is able to contribute.

- A range of ideas can be used.

Cons

- It can lead to confusion if not sensitively handled.

Research

There is nothing mysterious about research in this context, it means the same as elsewhere – finding out! How much you attempt to find out will depend on the style that you are aiming for in your drama.

Suppose you decided to go for a fully historical representation of the parable of the widow and the judge. You would clearly need to find out a lot about the time that the story is set in. In particular, the actors playing the two characters would need to research what it meant to be a widow or a judge at the time. Various elements of what is discovered will then find their way into the resulting characterization.

Research need not, of course, be directly related to the text. If you chose to move the parable into a different context (set it in the present day, for example), then it would be the new context that you might need to research. If the parable of the widow and the judge became the parable of the single parent and the DHSS, then you might need to research your new context, although you may, of course, have ample experience of either or both.

Research need not be dull and boring. If you're not the type for poring over books or looking up reference after reference, you can find ways to make research a practical learning experience. Some suggestions for this are given below.

Research – talk to people

Find a judge or magistrate (or any authority figure). Talk to them about their job. Find out what the particular stresses and tensions are. Do the same with someone who has a grievance. This need not be a major thing – it shouldn't be too hard to find someone who's had a lengthy battle with some sort of authority, garage, or book club! Again, let the person talk and try to understand what that situation feels like from the inside.

Research – make a mural

Get the group to agree research tasks and then ask them to bring relevant pictures, press cuttings, poems – in fact, anything that can be brought along to your next meeting. These are then stuck to the wall to form a mural. The whole point is that no one is expected to spend hours researching their topic, they just bring along whatever they see which might be of interest.

An individual who is looking at the judge might bring along press cuttings of court cases, pictures of legal types, or they might have devised a simple questionnaire to reveal the group's attitude to the courts and legal procedures. All of the research is stuck on the wall for the group to comment on and work from during the session.

Research – discuss

Discussion can be a form of research. You're researching each other's views and ideas. In order to research the character of the widow, for example, you might talk about your own experiences of persistently trying to achieve something or attempting to right a wrong. As suggested above, make notes on big sheets of paper of the chief points raised. It's important to try to get as open a discussion as possible. There should be the freedom for individuals to express their doubts as well as their certainties.

Situations

To help deepen a basic characterization, try putting that character in different situations. We recently worked with a group in Wiessach, West Germany, who had asked us to concentrate on characterization and also the use of movement. This notion of putting characters into different situations was one of the most productive of our workshop sessions. At the time we were working on the character of Pilate and as they worked together on short scenes showing Pilate at different stages of his life and in different situations, the resulting characterizations became much more rounded and believable.

The scenes that they worked on, included Pilate:

- With a subordinate
- With a superior
- With his wife
- Trying to impress someone

The scenes were not prepared to be shown to anyone, but were intended to give the actors something to focus on when experimenting with the character of Pilate. They concentrated on the differences in his behaviour in each situation, looking at such things as,

- How did Pilate enter the situation?
- What were his inner thoughts and feelings and how were these suggested?

Having worked on these situations, the actors, working in groups of two, were free to develop one of them into a longer scene which was shared with and discussed by the rest of the group.

The same principle of working can be applied to any script or passage that you are working from.

One way of choosing the situations to experiment with is to think of emotional states of the character that you wish to explore. Taking the widow as an example you might draw up a table something like this,

Emotion	Situation
■ Anger	■ Third attempt to see the judge and obtain a hearing
■ Hope	■ Discussion with a friend who encourages her to keep trying
■ Joy	■ The judge tells her that he will grant her request
■ Grief	■ When she hears of the death of her husband

You may feel that these examples are too dramatic for your group. If that is the case, then go for more mundane snippets of the widow's life such as,

- Meeting a friend at the market
- Having a dispute with a neighbour
- Her first explanation of her case to the judge

Let's return to the little drama that started this framework and see what differences the ideas in this chapter might make.

Scene one

The group arrives a few minutes early to assemble a mural of the week's research into the parable.

Scene two

After a quick warm up game (energetically led by Jim and Merry) and some exercises, the group study the mural made a few minutes earlier. They see images of courts and judges, of plaintiffs and justice. An energetic discussion ensues.

Scene three

You don't want to bring this exciting discussion to an end but, as director, you feel it is time to move into action. Large sheets of paper go up on the wall and the ideas from the discussion are jotted down. The list continues to grow as the session continues.

You start telling each other stories about the judge, then about the widow. As the ideas begin to build up you move into character endowment, the judge first and then the widow. James says that the judge is keen on Leviticus – he can quote the law but can't apply it fairly. This suggestion is taken on by Bob who says he would like to try some hot-seating. Molly prefers to be hot-seated with some others, so two group members join her for a session of many actors, one character.

Scene four

Everyone's getting really excited now so the group works in pairs, trying out the characters in different situations. After half an hour they choose one of these experiments and polish it for sharing. You look at each other's ideas. Molly and Bob say they now feel very confident in their characterizations. The group are so happy with things that they move straight into working out a lively, funny, pithy, and telling sketch based on the parable . . . and all because they started by really working on the characters!

Sounds too good to be true? Of course it does. If your group really went "by the book" like that they'd be so boring they'd never create anything! Perhaps think of the above as your "game plan". You never know, you might come close to it.

Before leaving characters we would like to stress, once again, that we have used one simple parable as an example of each of these ways of working. We really do not expect you to try out all these ideas just to create a sketch version of the widow and the judge. Indeed, if you did you'd probably end up with an impossibly over-worked piece.

19

Summary

If you use, adapt, and develop the ideas in this framework, you will have a number of ways of getting more out of your drama by focussing on characters. Here's a reminder of the basic ideas given.

■ Lists and notes	Keep records of ideas as they develop
■ Tell a story	A way of "fleshing out" a character's background
■ Hot-seating	Character under pressure Many actors, one character Symbolic character endowment
■ Research	Background information – relate to time and setting of piece. Discussion
■ Situations	Explore characters' reactions to different situations

The idea is that you take whatever ideas seem appropriate for whatever you're working on, but we would suggest doing some character development work regardless of how simple the passage or text is that you're working from. On the other hand, if you did choose to create a full-length play based on the widow and the judge you'd probably use most of the ideas in this book during your rehearsal period. Any takers?

The dramatic material which follows could all be developed and rehearsed using ideas from this framework.

Heavenly Dialogue *by Gordon Lamont*

Introduction

This is not a sketch about heaven! It uses the idea of heaven for its setting but it actually explores themes concerned with the way we live now. The sketch was inspired by the Gospel theme of the cost of discipleship – what it actually means to love God and your neighbour as yourself. *Heavenly Dialogue* tries to open up these themes in a very practical way.

Bible basis

■ Matthew 7.13–14 and Luke 13.24 — the narrow gate to life.

The sketch explores this through the notion that to follow Christ involves us in daily giving of ourselves in many small, seemingly trivial ways.

■ Matthew 25.31–40. Christ's words about who will be judged as righteous at the final judgement.

This is packed up in the sketch with its emphasis on what it means to be a disciple, to see Christ in all people, and to visit "him" when people are sick or in prison.

Production notes

More than any other piece in this book, *Heavenly Dialogue* depends on the text rather than humorous interpretation or the use of movement or mime. The props used are also essential to the message of the sketch.

Useful exercises

Hot-seating and endowment from the *Characters* framework might be useful (page 11), instant still images related to feelings from the *Still-image* framework (page 42) and adding thoughts from the *Dramatic tension* framework (page 65).

Props

■ Leaflet, hessian bag, wine flagon, bread, crown of thorns, large fish (not neccesarily naturalistic!)

Set

■ Park bench

Characters

Both characters can be either female or male. This is something to think about as you may find that the sketch says more or less, depending on the way that you cast with regard to race, gender, and age.

Barlow

Outspoken, confident in most situations, but feeling rather ill at ease during the dream part of the sketch.

Ward

Helpful, relaxed but with a sharp mind and wit. Age is

immaterial. Ward should be dressed in a comfortable style that suits the person playing the part.

Heavenly Dialogue

The stage is set with a bench. On the bench is a leaflet.

> *Enter Barlow.*
> *Barlow addresses the audience.*

Barlow   I read in the paper the other day that most of us don't remember most of the dreams we have. Well, maybe I do remember them, or maybe I don't, in which case there's nothing to remember. I did dream that I was a refrigerator once and I got sold to a woman with an enormous bag full of salted herring.

Perhaps it's just as well that I don't dream too often, or don't remember if I do. Anyway, last night I had a most vivid dream; there was a giraffe in it, a tandoori take-away, a gate that was very narrow, a distinct absence of music, and me – dead; (*sees the bench*) and oh yes, there was a park bench.

> *Barlow moves towards the bench and sits down, looking lost.*
> *He picks up the leaflet and begins to read it. He is clearly*
> *unhappy with what he reads.*

> *Enter Ward.*

Ward   Mind if I sit down and rest my legs a minute?
Barlow   Please do.
Ward   Is something the matter? You seem a bit lost.
Barlow   Well, I'm not really sure what to do.
Ward   Oh? Hasn't anyone given you a job?
Barlow   Er, I'm not sure. I think I've just arrived and I don't really know what to do.
Ward   Oh heavens, no pun intended. Surely you know. You just have to ask here and anyone will be delighted to help you.
Barlow   Oh, right. The thing is . . . well . . .
Ward   What is it?
Barlow   Well, to tell the truth, it's not at all how I imagined it.

I say, that day was a bit of a laugh!

Oh, I mustn't forget those silvery things, flapping about in all that wet stuff . . . There were loads of them. I don't know how they could hold their breath for so long.

But anyway, the Lord God declared that it was good.

Well, we all found a few twigs and settled down for a nice night's kip; well, all apart from a couple of insomniac owls.

But what an awakening . . . Loud? Baying! Snorting! Neighing! Barking! They were everywhere, all – ready for this? – walking! Not a pair of wings between 'em . . . just legs. They had really funny feathers as well . . . all thin, but loads of them.

I might say that night we found some twigs a bit higher up and settled down for another sleep . . . I'm sure someone's going to end up strangling those owls!

Next day the "leggies" (as we called 'em) were still there . . . but so were the last of the Lord's little "masterpieces". I'm sorry, but he got it wrong this time . . . not only no wings, but no feathers as well! All pre-plucked; there they were, as bald as you like, strutting around on . . . *two* legs! Why? They'd been given four . . . so why not use 'em?

Totally impractical design if you ask me . . . Still, we trust in the wisdom of the Lord. But I must say that we, or The Amalgamated Union of Predatory, Migratory, and Horn-Billed Birds, were a touch miffed that so-called "man" was put in charge . . . Even so far as naming the rest of us. I apparently am an American Bald Eagle . . . Thinning maybe . . . bald never!

Hello? Where's Black Headed Mamba off to? Another one with no wings and no fur. Oooh, aren't we high and mighty, mixing with the woman . . . Well, I should steer clear of him if I were you, love. He'll only lead you up the garden path . . . Talking of which, where do they think they're going?

Here, you can't go up there . . . That's the Tree of Knowledge . . . You're forbidden to eat that, that's forbidden fruit . . . Oh, oh. That's it, she's done it now . . . When the Lord God finds out . . . Well . . . at least man hasn't eat . . . Where's she going with that?

She wouldn't . . .
Well, he wouldn't
She would, and he has.

Well, that's just typical . . . One simple instruction from the Lord their God, and who are the only ones to disobey it? His favourites! Hmph!

Of course, there wouldn't be this trouble if they had wings . . . small ones even . . . and just a few feathers.

Fade

(*A Peck at Paradise* is part of the show . . . *If They Had Wings* first performed by Stripes Theatre Company.)

Jonah *by Stephen Deal*

Introduction

This presentation explores human reactions when God calls people for difficult tasks. It focuses on Jonah and uses the monologue form to give his perspective on the events. It is a less cosy piece than *A Peck at Paradise* (page 29); defensive, and at times belligerent, with Jonah putting questions directly to the audience to consider about accepting or rejecting God's commands. It is a less easy piece, too, and requires careful rehearsal and variation to achieve its effects.

Bible basis
- Jonah 1–4

Production notes

Character

Jonah is a character who feels hard done by. He has tried to avoid God's call and attempts to justify his actions, but struggles to understand the forgiveness of sinners (Nineveh). The actor could use actions and movements to indicate different parts of the story, and use a different voice for the lines spoken by God. Costume could be plain or more realistically biblical, but white hair is necessary for the effect. A sandal is all that is required as a prop. Full use should be made of the space available (designating various areas as ship, whale, Nineveh, etc.), and of the various dramatic climaxes (Jonah's conversations with God, the storm, and his various complaints).

Useful exercises

Hot-seating, symbol as character, and character under pressure would be useful exercises in preparing for this piece, and the section on monologues (page 26) gives more general help on this type of performance.

Jonah

The lights come up on Jonah, sitting under a palm tree, mending a sandal.

My name is Jonah . . . Yes, that Jonah . . . The "Swallowed by a Big Fish" Jonah . . . The "I bet he had a whale of a time" "Jonah. Very funny. Ha, Ha. Do you see me laughing? Do you think I enjoy being the joke of the Bible? You hear them say . . . "And the story of Jonah just goes to show that you can't run away from God." Then everyone closes their Bibles and says, "Silly old Jonah, if he'd only done what he'd been told life would have been so much easier!"

Well, it wasn't that simple.

There I was, sat at home making sandals . . . Oh, and keeping one eye on my father, Amittai, who's getting on a bit, and tends to wander off and buy camels, if you let him. Suddenly, the Word of the Lord comes to me. No real problem there . . . except I managed to sew a piece of leather onto my thumb in surprise . . .

"Jonah," the voice said, "Jonah"
"I heard you the first time!" I said.
"Don't get touchy," said the voice, "I've got a job for you."

Well, I had a look to see if anyone was having a joke at Jonah's expense. Found that Amittai had slipped away to buy camel food, so I was totally alone . . .

"Jonah," said the voice again. "Don't waste my time, there's work to be done."
"You want some sandals mended?" I asked.

"Don't be facetious," says the Lord. "I want you to go to Nineveh and preach against its wickedness."

"You've got to be joking, O Lord," I replied. "The people of

33

Nineveh are vicious and evil. Do you know the tortures they inflict on their enemies? I can't go there."

"Want to bet?" says the Lord.

Well, you know what happened next. I very sensibly hopped on the first boat going to Tarshish – which is about as far away from Nineveh as you can get. No way was I going to that hell-hole.

Anyway, I was asleep down-stairs – sorry, "below-decks" – when the Lord blew up this terrific storm, and it looks at though the boat I'm on is going to sink. The sailors start to throw the cargo overboard, in an attempt to lighten the ship – but to no avail. Then they start praying to their gods . . . still nothing happens. Eventually the captain comes down and wakes me up.

Now notice that I said, "Wakes me up" . . . Because I'm asleep. During a raging storm, I, Jonah, am asleep! Why am I asleep? Because I've a clear conscience, that's why. Because I did not feel guilty about not going to Nineveh. Because I knew I was doing the right thing in disobeying God.

Well, the captain says to me: "Get up and pray to your god. Maybe he will hear your prayer and have mercy on us."

Meanwhile, the crew have been drawing lots to decide whose fault the situation was – guess who copped the short straw! I told them; it was God's fault for being angry with me for not doing what he wanted . . . I also told them the best way out of the mess was to throw me overboard. Well, it was me God wanted, not them, and the sooner I was off the ship, the sooner he would leave them alone.

Fair's fair, they tried to get me ashore but the Lord is creator of the winds and the seas . . . and he was having none of it. So in the end they had to bung me into the briny deep. Straight away the sea goes calm, but by then it's too late, I'm in the water . . . and since there's not much call for it in sandal making, I can't swim – so I'm drowning . . . Drowning and praying and shouting, "Okay, okay Lord, you win. I think you're wrong but okay I'll go. I don't want to drown."

Now we get to the bit of my story that everybody thinks they know . . . I was swallowed by a big fish. "Jonah," people say to me, "Jonah, was it a fish, or was it a whale . . . and if it was a whale . . . what kind?"

What a stupid question . . . within half a second I was inside the thing . . . What am I, a marine biologist that I can identify a fish from the design of its stomach? It was wet and cramped and smelly and generally disgusting. I say to the Lord, "Oh, thanks a lot!"

And he says, "What do you expect in the middle of an ocean at such short notice . . . a cabin with steward service maybe? Be serious Jonah. Now go to Nineveh and preach against its wickedness!"

I might say I spent the next three days in fervent prayer – well quite frankly I didn't like the idea of the Lord changing his mind and leaving me inside the belly of some fish like a kind of exotic stuffing.

Then suddenly – Ugh! The fish, or whale or whatever, vomits me up on this beach, and the word of the Lord comes to me again and says, "Go to the great city of Nineveh and proclaim to it the message I give to you".

So off I went.

Now, Nineveh is a big city. It takes three days to walk across it. I had to go right to the centre with the message that in forty days' time the city would be destroyed. People took notice of me because – I was the colour of snow. The acids in the fish's stomach had bleached my skin and my hair white. I think the people took one look at me and said: "Hey, his god scares him so much he's turned white!" – You bet they took notice! And very soon the whole city had repented, and everyone was very happy. Well I wasn't! I was so mad I could spit!

Now we get to the part of my story that really puzzles people – why was I mad at the Lord?

Was it because I was afraid to go to Nineveh and get myself killed? No. I knew I could trust in the Lord for protection.

Was it because I'd gone into Nineveh preaching death and destruction in forty days' time, and that nothing was going to happen when the deadline passed? That I'd been made to look a fool? No. Any prophet should be glad that the people hear the Word of God and repent.

No, the reason I was mad at God was because I knew that when the Ninevites repented he would have mercy on them and forgive them. And that seemed unjust to me. The Ninevites were scum. They were evil in every sense of the word.

They hurled their enemies down on to spikes in pits. They killed women and children . . . by torture.

It was as if the Lord had said to you, as you sat there, thinking what an old fool Jonah is . . . "Go to the guards, the captains, the commandants, who ran the concentration camps in your Second World War" – men who killed millions of Jews and gypsies and people who just didn't fit into their scheme of things – "and say to them, 'Repent and you will be forgiven'". And to know that they would hear your voice and repent and that God would forgive them the evil they had done, and they would escape the punishment they deserved. And because of a message that you had carried to them. How could you look your Jewish friend in the eye again? It would be better that you were dead. That is how I felt. I said to the Lord, "I want to die!"

The trouble with God is that he is very difficult to be mad at. What do you do? Throw stones at him? Scream and shout? Me? I sulked. He had used me to do something I did not want to do. What did he expect. A cheery wave and a shout of "anytime"?

I built a shelter and sat down to watch the fate of the city. I already knew in my heart that it would be spared, but I wanted to see for myself. It was very hot and the sun was very bright. The Lord caused a vine to grow next to me and give me shade – "Hello," I said. "Things are looking up; perhaps the Lord does care about how I feel – doesn't want me to suffer."

However, my comfort was short-lived, as next day the Lord sent a worm to destroy the vine and I was back at being mad with him again. He seemed to be teasing me. Offering comfort and then stealing it away. I was very angry. I felt messed about. That vine was mine, for my comfort.

Then God said to me:

"Do you have a right to be angry about that vine?"
Well, I told him. I said, "I do. I am angry enough to die." I meant it too. I was at the end of my tether.

Then God said to me: "You have been concerned about this vine though you did not tend it or make it grow. It sprang up overnight, and died overnight. But Nineveh has more than one hundred and twenty thousand people who cannot tell their right hand from their left. Should I not be concerned with that great city?"

What could I say? I said nothing. If God chooses to forgive any-one, who am I, a sandal-maker, to argue? I still feel uncomfortable that his forgiveness extends to those I would consider unforgivable . . . but he is the Lord, and I am his servant.

When I got back home, I had another mess to sort out. In my enforced absence my dotty old father had managed to buy thirty-seven camels. Oi! No wonder I've got the hump!

When I got back home, I had another mess to sort out. In my enforced absence my dotty old father had managed to buy thirty-seven camels. Oi! No wonder I've got the hump!

Lights start a slow fade.

Well, what do you expect? Humour from a man who spends his time in the belly of a fish?

Total fade.

(*Jonah* is from the show . . . *If They Had Wings*, first performed by Stripes Theatre Company)

Kenan and Son (or "Not so much a canoe . . .") *by Stephen Deal*

Introduction

The story of Noah is one of the best known in the Bible, and there are many treatments of it. This monologue concentrates on the imagination of Noah's task and the attitudes of other people to its seeming stupidity. It looks at making a fool of oneself for God, with the audience's knowledge of who has the last laugh. The piece would work well in a children's context or church service. Unlike the other two presentations in this form, Caleb does not address the audience directly but speaks to Noah by phone, and shouts comments to his father who is offstage. This allows more scope for comedy and creates a less intimate situation with the audience.

Bible basis
- Genesis 6

Production notes

Character

Caleb is a cheerful character, willing to please but who has problems grasping large or abstract concepts. He could believe himself to be quite a crafty and confident salesman but is thrown by Noah's order.

The character needs a convincing manner, with pauses for Noah's imagined replies and careful timing of the links between the phone dialogue and offstage contact with his father.

There is little movement, so expression and gesture are particularly important. Simple costume is probably most appropriate here (an apron) with a few props: telephone, order pad and pencil, and slide rule.

Useful exercises

Research (page 16) – discussion on the topic of Noah's task or of making a fool of oneself for God could help the approach to this piece. See also the note on monologues (page 26).

Kenan and Son (or "Noah on the blower")

A phone rings and Caleb goes to answer it, wearing a carpenter's apron.

Hello? Kenan and Son, Carpenters and timber merchants. Caleb speaking. Yes guv' . . . you wish to place an order. Right you are. One second while I get my order pad.

He hunts around for his order pad.

Right then. Can I have your name . . . Noah, son of Lamech. Address? . . . Top of the hill, turn right . . . gotcha. Okay then, what can we do you for? Oh, you're not exactly sure of the quantity of timber? Well, what do you want it for? Perhaps we can work it out . . . An ark . . . I see. Er . . . what exactly is an ark? Sorry, thought you said a kind of boat. Oh, you did. How big do you want this boat? Sorry . . . ark? . . . 300 cubits long . . . 50 cubits wide . . . and 30 cubits high. Hang on a mo' – we work in metric here, I'll have to do the conversions, where's me slide-rule?

He carries out a complex equation on the slide rule.

Let's see. Carry the one, shift the decimal point two places, multiply by . . . no divide by . . . oh, let's say four, no that can't be right, make it sixteen and seven eighths. Hang on mate, I won't be long. It's so much easier dealing in metric, 'lot simpler . . . Translate along the x-axis . . . Do you know the cosine of eleven? Oh right. And there we have it!

He looks proudly at the piece of paper. Then puzzled. He looks at the slide rule, and then hastily recalculates a bit.

That was 300 cubits, wasn't it, mate? Yeah? Sorry, I must have got the decimal point in the wrong place – only I make your boat 140 metres long . . . which is a bit big for the local pond, don't you think? Oh . . . it sounds about right to you . . . Going sailing in our bath were we sir? . . . Do I want the order or not – yes, I want the order. One moment . . .

He covers the receiver and shouts offstage.

Dad! Dad! There's a bloke here wants to build a boat . . . no, not so much a canoe . . . more yer' luxury liner . . . What?

To Noah.

Where do you intend building this boat . . . sorry, ark?

To his father.

In his back garden. No, you can't even see the stream, let alone the sea! . . . I'll ask.

To Noah.

Mr Noah? My father is a little curious about how you intend to get your boat to the sea . . . I mean perhaps we can help . . . you're going to need a lot of people pushing . . . God. No, I don't think I know him – is he a boat builder?

Oh, more of a Grand Architect, I see. And what's his role in this very interesting little project?

He's going to make it rain . . . Well . . . that'll keep us cool anyway . . . It's going to rain so hard that the "ark" will float away . . . I'd better get the washing in then hadn't I?

Of course I'm taking you seriously! After all, all you want to do is build a large ship in the middle of a desert and wait for this "God" to make it rain and float the thing away in the puddles. This will be cash in advance, won't it?

Okay, okay . . . I was just asking. We've got a living to make . . . You'll mortgage your house, and we'll hold on to the

deeds. Well that seems fairly secure. Now, this is going to take a lot of wood . . . By the way . . . what sort of wood do you want? . . . One that floats . . .
. . . Cyprus Wood . . I can do you a good deal in four-ply . . .
. . . It's got to be Cyprus Wood.
Mr Noah . . . if you don't mind me asking . . . why do you want a ship in the middle of the desert? A novel idea for a restaurant is it?
. . . You're going to fill it with animals. What, like a zoo?
. . . Oh . . . Why?
. . . To stop them drowning when it rains. So it's going to be more than a brief shower then . . . more like a deluge – But if these animals need rescuing, what about us humans?
. . . What do you mean, "exactly"?
. . . Oh, yes I understand you have a family to look after. I mean you wouldn't want them getting their feet wet, would you? The rest of us have to make do with wellies, I suppose. And when can we expect this deluge to occur then?
. . . When you finish building the ark . . .

To his father.

Dad, don't hurry this order . . .

To Noah.

Now, may I suggest you take your time, sir . . . It's bad to rush a job as tricky as an ark . . . Arks are very time-consuming things to build. In fact I don't recall anyone ever finishing one before.

Right. We'll get this order together for you, and send it up when it's ready. You'd better start organizing those animals . . . Oh, my cousin Ibraim owns a pet shop . . . He could do you a good deal in hamsters and white mice.
. . . Oh, right. Well, it's been a pleasure doing business with you, sir; bye then.

He puts the phone down and addresses his father while he fills the order in on the pad.

'Ere Dad! This Noah bloke really reckons that God is going to flood the world and wipe us all out . . . What do you think?
. . . Relocate the business? . . . Good idea . . . better make it somewhere high. I know . . . Mount Ararat.

Fade.

(*Kenan and Son* is from the show . . . *If They Had Wings,* first performed by Stripes Theatre Company)

4. Still Images Framework

In the Kinetik Theatre production *In a City*, we told the story of the ministers of two inner-city churches and their approaches to ministry. Sounds boring doesn't it! We hope it wasn't, and one of the ways that we developed for exploring this theme was that of a tension between the two characters involved. This tension was based on their ideological differences and his romantic designs on her. Here's a short extract from one of the scenes, set in a restaurant.

David   . . . and so, to the restaurant. For starters?
Jean   Grapefruit juice – unsweetened.
David   Stuffed mushrooms – sweetened with light conversation about my arrival in the parish.

Tableau

Jean   Main course?
David   Chicken provencale, and vegetables of the day, delicately seasoned with polite but supportive discussion of your work.
Jean   Vegetable mornay.
David   With?
Jean   A side salad. Aside from which I get the distinct impression that all this is leading us somewhere . . .

Tableau

David   Dessert?
Jean   Not for me, thanks.
David   I think . . . ah yes, the cheese board. The mature cheddar, and you know Jean, I think it's time for mellow and mature memories of our student days.

What we are interested in here are the tableaux. Tableaux are simply still images made by the actors "freezing". There is an old form of entertainment in which people create different tableaux with a curtain pulled across between the scenes. That is a rather clumsy way of using the strategy although it can be good fun at boring parties. In the brief extract above, you will see that still images are used to highlight what's going on. The action is stopped for a count of five and the audience gets a chance to reflect on what's happening. We often found, when playing this scene, that the audience laughed at David's attempts at intimacy with Jean and her attempts to resist this, but the important point is that those laughs came with the tableaux. We were in just the same positions as we had been a second before, but the opportunity to stop and consider and reflect on what was going on revealed the humour in the situation because the audience was able to understand better exactly what the characters were up to.

The use of still images can be very powerful, both in a finished piece of theatre and as a means of exploring the piece during rehearsal. Let's take a Bible passage and explore it using still images.

This time we'll take a well-known Old Testament story, the death of Samson from Judges 16.

> The Philistine kings met together to celebrate and offer a great sacrifice to their god dagon. They sang, "Our god has given us victory over our enemy Samson!" They were enjoying themselves, so they said, "Call Samson, and let's make him entertain us!" When they brought Samson out of the prison, they made him entertain them and made him stand between the pillars. When the people saw him, they sang praise to their god: "Our god has given us victory over our enemy, who devastated our land and killed so many of us!" Samson said to the boy who was leading him by the hand, "Let me touch the pillars that hold up the building. I want to lean on them. The building was crowded with men and women. All five Philistine kings were there, and there were about three thousand men and women on the roof, watching Samson entertain them.
>
> (Judges 16.23–27)

We can stop the story at this point and explore this section using still images. As in other frameworks, what follows is not so much a workshop session for you to follow from the book, as the use of a particular passage to explain the various strategies that can be employed when using still images.

One of the simplest and most useful ways of using this framework in rehearsals or workshops is to get the group (or work in small groups if you have enough people) to tell the story using a limited number of still images. We would suggest four or five images for the above section of the story. This has two major benefits:

■ The group will get to know the details of the story quickly and in a practical manner.

■ They will begin to consider the significant points of the story (for more on this, see the dramatic tension framework on page 65).

In order to keep the group "on their toes" during this exercise, feed in the following at what you judge to be the appropriate points.

■ Don't allow the use of any furniture or props. Everything has to be made with the actor's own bodies. This could include the furniture, the pillars, and the roof!

■ Call out titles related to the passage which the group have to quickly portray as still images, without discussion amongst themselves. Suitable titles might include, the Philistine kings, the crowd, the image of Dagon, Samson in prison, singing praise to Dagon, and the entertainment.

■ Give just a single-word title which the group have to interpret instantly, as above. Use feeling-related words such as darkness, mockery, or prisoner.

■ Try an image with all the actors being the same character but represented at different times in the story. The most obvious candidate is Samson and this might really help to get under the skin of his feelings and thoughts.

Before going on, it's good to remind ourselves that the above are given as ways of getting into and understanding the situation, although the results of such exercises might find their way into a finished piece of theatre in some form. The example given is necessarily based on a short extract from the whole story and, when working on any story, you will want to explore the whole even if you only plan to present a part. All of the exercises given can be used to look at the story of Samson from start to finish.

Now let's add some more of the story and work on that, looking at how we can work towards a performance with still images at its heart.

Then Samson prayed, "Sovereign LORD, please remember me; please, God, give me my strength just once more, so that with this one blow I can get even with the Philistines for putting out my two eyes." So Samson took hold of the two middle pillars holding up the building. Putting one hand on each pillar, he pushed against them and shouted, "Let me die with the Philistines!" He pushed with all his might, and the building fell down on all five kings and everyone else. Samson killed more people at his death than he had killed during his life.

(Judges 16.28–30)

In many ways this story is a gift for using still images because it is very graphic and visual.

If you are going to use still images in performance then there are a number of basics to bear in mind.

Still image basics

■ A still image should look like "frozen action", not just like a group of people hanging around in awkward poses. Think of your image as a photograph. The action is "caught", the expressions are held (a half-formed smile remains half formed), a dog cocking its leg is forever interrupted in the moment before relief (and whoever is playing the lamp-post needs to stand firm as only a lamp-post can).

■ A still image should be interesting to look at. Go for different levels, not just everyone standing up or sitting down. When you are re-organizing and refining your image for performance, think of it as a painter would treat a canvas. Look at all parts of the image in relation to all other parts. Is the image exciting or thought provoking to look at? Most importantly, does the whole thing work together to say what you want it to say?

■ Think of where the audience will be in relation to the image. Will they be looking from just one side, as in an "end-on" performance, from two sides (transverse), from three sides (arena or thrust) or will the performance be "in the round"? You might also consider a performance where the audience are free to wander around the images as if they were sculpture. Wherever your audience will be, you need to think of what they will see and structure your work with that in mind.

■ Learn to concentrate. This is basic and very important for still images. One giggler or two roving eyes will destroy the look of your carefully constructed image. Still images may be a simple technique, but they require as much commitment as other forms of acting.

■ Use the power and clarity of still images to help your audience reflect on what you understand to be the central issue(s) of the passage. In this case is it about God hearing Samson? Is it about

Samson giving himself for what he believes in, or has the passage more to do with someone who has suffered and is at the limit of endurance? You'll have to talk and, more importantly, work this through with your group.

Refining the image

These important ground rules can be applied to any use of still images, so let's move on to build a drama around this passage using them.

■ As before, tell the story using just enough images to give the essence. This time really work on the images. Try moving people around to get the most satisfying and graphic pictures. Individuals can come out of a picture to look at it, one at a time. If you are working with a director, they can take each individual's place to give a better idea of the whole, but this is not essential as each person who steps out to look will have a clear idea of their own position and pose. If you are serious about using still images, you will want to work on them for quite a while to achieve really telling results.

■ Now see what happens when you try to add sound to the pictures. See what can be achieved by creating the sounds of the Philistine revels. Perhaps you will create a really effective contrast between the revels and the moment when Samson prays, which brings us on to the next stage . . .

■ Try using some speech in your piece. We would strongly advise keeping this to a minimum so as not to detract from the power of the images that you have spent so long working on. A quotation from the passage might be useful to set the scene, depending, of course, on what the context of the performance is. If the drama is to be part of a Bible reading in church then the scene may well have been set already. Samson's prayer may be really effective, as the only spoken section in a drama otherwise made up of images and sounds. As with so much in this book, this is where your judgement and creativity will have to take over to use the framework in the most appropriate manner.

■ See what can be achieved by adding movement to your images. We are not in any sense talking about undoing the impact of your images by "bringing them to life". The basic aim when using this framework is to go for the clarity that still images give. Nevertheless, it is possible in some circumstances to enhance that clarity with some movement.

Try creating three images of the pillars being pushed apart and then running them closely together to create a film-frame effect. You may feel that adding movement in this way detracts from the effect you have created with your images, but even so, you will have to find a way of going from one image to another. This will inevitably involve movement, so it is worth experimenting with ways of making the movement fit the nature of the image.

■ Having worked on images, sounds, speech, and movement, you are now in a position to look at what you've achieved and begin to polish it for performance. As we said in "Basics", above, working on a passage in this way will inevitably throw up all sorts of questions about what it has to say to you and to your audience. In other words, why are you presenting this particular drama based on this particular passage (apart from the fact that the minister has asked you to and you're after them for funds for your budding dance and drama group)?

Give emphasis to the questions that you feel this passage raises. One example of this might be if you wanted to stress the idea that the Lord heard Samson and acted with him. Then you could create a focus on that particular moment of the story by skilful use of sound and silence, still image and movement. This might take the form of an image of Samson looking to God for help, an image which you hold just longer than the audience is expecting before Samson's strength is renewed and the image bursts into powerful life.

See what the effect is of returning to that particular image at the end of your presentation, so that when the story is over the audience is returned to one significant image from it.

Summary

Let's look briefly at the ideas suggested in this framework:

Tell a story

■ Use still images to break the story up into pictures. This will help you really get to know the story and to identify significant moments.

Use bodies as things

■ Get the creative juices flowing by denying the use of props.

Instant pictures

■ Think fast (and clearly!) to create an image to fit a title or explore a feeling.

Add sounds and words

■ Use these sparingly to support rather than swamp your images.

Add movement

■ Look at how you move between images.

Before leaving this framework, you might like to think about how to apply these still-image techniques to existing scripts. We started with an extract from *In a City*, which used this strategy. See if you can apply it usefully to any of the scripts which follow. The most obvious use is as a freeze to start and finish scenes, but also consider it as a useful way of adding emphasis.

Traveller Casserole *by Gordon Lamont*

Introduction

This simple dramatic version of the well-known parable of the good Samaritan is based on an idea developed at a workshop which we led in Sheffield. We looked at various parts of the Bible and encouraged the workshop group to come up with dramatic approaches that helped to expose the material rather than simply adding unnecessary complication as so much improvisation does. We were looking for a concept for the drama which would hold an audience's interest and not obscure the meaning inherent in the original passage. One group decided to look at the parable of the good Samaritan and came up with the excellent idea of telling the story as a recipe.

Traveller Casserole uses that same basic idea and we are grateful to Isobel Atkinson, Heather Burgin, Justine Leesley, and David Hinchcliffe who worked out the original sketch.

Bible basis

■ Luke 10.30–37

Production notes

There have been a number of dramatic versions of this parable, perhaps the best known being the Riding Lights' *Parable of the Good Punk Rocker*. That particular version is so good because it makes abundantly clear Jesus' point that the good was done by someone who would not be expected to behave well, while the "good" characters did nothing. That important point must come across if you present this sketch, and you will rely heavily on the Cook to convey it with the certainty that as an ingredient the Samaritan is simply inferior. The Cook is the only speaking part in the sketch and this makes it ideal for a first attempt at public performance. The sketch's simplicity means than an inexperienced group can produce good results.

The sketch assumes that the audience are for the most part familiar with the parable and is specifically designed to overcome some of the problems caused by such familiarity. We would advise simplicity in the presentation of the piece. It should appear to your audience as a novel approach to the passage and one which does not detract from it. The metaphor of ingredients in a recipe will break down if there is too much "business" between the characters.

Useful exercises

The still images framework will give you some ideas for staging, particularly if when you come to work on *Traveller Casserole* you prepare an image of each new character and incident in the sketch that makes an interesting, funny, and clear picture of what is going on. Then use these pictures as the starting point for your action as you rehearse. You may find that the images find their way into the finished piece or that they simply get things going in rehearsal. Either way, we think they'll be useful to you as you work on *Traveller Casserole*.

Characters

■ Cook

Ingredients

■ Traveller
■ Three Robbers
■ Priest
■ Levite

- Samaritan
- Innkeeper

All characters can be female or male. Clever staging and quick changes would make it possible to have the same actors playing the parts of the robbers and other ingredients.

Traveller Casserole

The stage is set with a table laid for a cookery demonstration downstage right.

Enter Cook

Cook   Hello and welcome to "Cooking the Book" – your weekly Bible barbeque of divine dishes. This week, an old favourite. A tasty, nourishing meal with quite a kick once it's gone down – Traveller Casserole. Now for the ingredients. Take one well-seasoned traveller . . .

Enter traveller dressed in hiking gear with a backpack, binoculars, etc. Traveller walks purposefully to centre stage, full of the joys of hiking.

Cook   Add a handful of dust, some flies, and apply fierce heat.

As each of the above is mentioned the traveller becomes more and more weary. By the end the traveller is mopping the brow, swatting flies, and sinking down.

Cook   Now add a sprinkling of robbers . . .
Robbers pounce on from various unexpected places. They should wear good robber attire – striped vests, masks, etc. They surround the traveller and look menacing.
Cook   (with clinical precision) Beat well.

This calls for a brief, well-rehearsed mugging. The effect should be of arms and legs flying out of a general bundle of people with appropriate "argghh" type noises. Beano fans will know the sort of thing.

Cook	Before the traveller is overdone, remove the robbers.
	Robbers begin to exit hastily.
Cook	*(interrupting their exit)* And pick the carcass clean. *Robbers return and remove camera, binoculars, money, etc. Exit robbers.*
Cook	Bake in the hot sun until only a little life remains. At this point you have Pureed Pedestrian. A pleasant dish but one which you might like to improve with one of the following exotic ingredients to produce a truly remarkable Traveller Casserole. You might try a pious priest. You can get these pickled but they have difficulty standing up so I've selected a good, firm, positively pious example and it just so happens that I have one ready prepared, to save time.
	Enter priest, who walks slowly toward the traveller with head held high as the cook speaks.
Cook	We all know that delicate aroma of holiness and I'm sure that this Traveller Casserole will be enhanced by the addition of this fine ingredient.
	The priest has reached the traveller, stops, and moves haughtily away to the other side of the stage. Priest freezes in characteristic pose with back to audience.
Cook	You may feel however that the fine bouquet of piety that the priest exudes is altogether too admirable for this humble dish and it might be better, on reflection, to move the priest to the other side of the pan. That being so, can I suggest that we try a little Levite – expensive I know, but such an unusual flavour.
	Enter Levite. The Levite is in a hurry, all of a fluster, nearly tripping over the traveller and quickly retreating to stand with the priest in a pose that shows distaste.
Cook	Well, perhaps not. Maybe the unusual flavour is just too fussy for this dish. There's really only one alternative if the priest and the Levite don't mix well with our traveller. If you really must, then I suppose you could

try just a sprinkling of Samaritan. Of course, they're not really in season – ever. You'll have to wash it thoroughly, and generally these curious little ingredients do not mix at all well. In fact, any day now they are going to prove that even a small quantity can lead to obesity and severe weight loss, hypertension, and drowsiness. They are really only safe with lots of dietary fibre and bags of unrefined sugar. However, we could just drop one in, and see what happens.

Enter Samaritan. The Samaritan is enjoying his walk, sees the traveller, and goes straight over.

Cook   And remove immediately.

Samaritan kneels down by traveller.

Cook   Remove immediately!

Samaritan takes out wine and pours some into the traveller's mouth.

Cook   (*flustered*) Alternatively, you could always add a little wine.

Samaritan begins to bandage traveller's arm.

Cook   (*regaining composure*) And dress for serving.

Samaritan helps the traveller up, and they move to the innkeeper who meets them stage left.

Cook   Finally, garnish with an innkeeper, a bag of money, and comfortable bed. Leave to marinade overnight.

During the above the traveller is handed over to the innkeeper and the bag of money exchanged. They freeze at the end of the above speech.

Cook   And there you have it, a tasty meal suitable for everyone – but it does need thoroughly digesting. This delightful meal is best served with a troubled conscience, and you can find the detailed recipe in the book *(holds up Bible)* which contains many other exciting recipes. Thank you.

All Exit. The Bible is left open on the Cook's table.

The Parable of the Talents *by Gordon Lamont*

Introduction

This sketch was originally part of the Kinetik Theatre production, *Refuge*. This one-act play with dance told the story of Jane Best, a convert to Christianity who finds it difficult to reconcile her personal faith with the suffering that she sees in the world – particularly in relation to refugees.

It is in Jane's nature to go on asking difficult questions rather than accept platitudes, so she joins the church drama group to help her to work through her new faith in a creative fashion. The parable of the talents is one of the group's sketches and it helps Jane to realize that she has a responsibility to use her questioning nature, not to bury it.

When performing this piece as part of *Refuge*, we were in the position of being a theatre company acting as a church drama group who were performing a sketch with three drama groups in it!

Bible basis

■ This sketch is based on Matthew 25.14–30.

Your audience will probably not realize this until the end because the sketch uses the idea of three church drama groups which are working on the parable of the sower. The analogy is drawn between the talents in the story (money) and the talents of the three groups (abilities).

Production notes

Number of performers

In *Refuge* we performed this sketch with three live performers (one for each drama group) and two on tape (Narrator and Minister). However, it would clearly still work well with five performers (with one actor representing each drama group) or more (if you represented each group by more than one actor). The piece is written so that the lines can easily be split to accommodate this.

Useful exercises

You should aim for a snappy, crisp presentation of this piece. Have a go at creating some really interesting and lively looking images around this sketch and find a way to move from one to another that maintains the pace of the piece. Look at *Adding movement*, *Instant pictures*, and *Tell the story*, all from *Still images*. Some of these images may well find their way into your finished version of the sketch. You might also like to look at some of the ideas in the *Characters* framework – perhaps some light-hearted hot-seating?

Characters

Narrator

■ Straight, dependable, and honest, but with a touch of earthy realism – facial expression comments on the action.

Minister

■ For once, not a buffoon, the minister is quite shrewd. Build in lots of knowing glances between minister and narrator.

Dancers

■ What will liturgical dance mean to your audience? If you know a well-respected local group, you may be able to pay them the compliment of sending them up without hard feelings. If this would be treading on too many toes, go for exaggerated seriousness and much, waffly arm waving (that should strike a chord somewhere – sounds a bit like a Kinetik production).

Improvisers

■ You're on much safer ground here as everyone will recognize the "imagine you're a tree" type of drama. Go for enthusiasm and naivety.

Script group

■ Serious, intense, self-opinionated – you must have met them.

The Parable of the Talents

Enter Narrator.

The narrator adopts a position from which he commands a view of the whole acting area and the audience. If you are performing in a church, the pulpit would be an ideal spot.

Narrator   There was once a church that had three drama groups.

                  Enter drama groups. They are protesting loudly at this idea.

Groups   Three! That's ridiculous. Don't make me laugh. A church with three drama groups? Pull the other one . . . *etc, etc.*

Narrator   *(interrupting them)* All right, all right. One dance group.

                  The dance group perform a brief dance with plastic smiles and much arm waving. This ends in a wet "praise" pose which is held.

Narrator   One improvisation group.

                  The improvisation group leap into action. One speaks while the rest of the group perform with much enthusiasm. If the group is played by just one person, the dance and script people do the actions at the behest of the improvisation person.

Improvisation   OK everyone, imagine you're a tree.

                  They form into intense, growing, twisted trees then freeze.

Improvisation   A family tree.

                  The group reform to present a victorian family portrait.

Narrator   And one script group.

*Intense studying of scripts from which the following
lines emerge.*

Script   Enter upstage left. Walk to centre stage. Look
                purposefully around. Turn. Exit downstage
                right. This is going to be our greatest production,
                I can feel it.
Narrator   The minister had to go away a few days so she
                left the three groups to prepare Sunday
                evening's sermon.

                *Enter minister. She is carrying a suitcase. The three
                groups reform. They are attentive and formal.*

Minister   You're to do the parable of the sower.
Narrator   Said the minister.
Minister   Dance group, you do the seed that fell on good
                soil.
Dance   Oooh great, can't wait.

                Dancers freeze in an excited pose.

Minister   Improvisation, the seed the birds ate.
Improvisation   Great part, can't wait to start.

                They freeze.

Minister   Script group, you're to take the seed that fell
                among thorns.
Script   Wonderful, what a love you are. What implica-
                tions, such didactic diversity. I see it in blue, the
                tabs rise, the scenery flies, the lights crossfade,
                the audience awaits, hushed, expectant, the
                music builds to a crescendo . . . or should
                we go for pathos, or bathos . . . oh, I see it
                all . . . the roar of the greasepaint, the smell
                of the crowd . . .
Narrator   *(interrupting)* So the minister set off.
Script   Please love! We're busy.
Narrator   The minister set off.

                Exit minister.

Narrator   And the three groups set to work.

56

Dance	And one, two, three, four, five, six, seven, eight . . . and down, two, three, four, and side, two, three, four and . . .

They freeze.

Improvisation	OK everyone . . . Remember . . . I don't care if the audience can't hear what you're saying, as long as they can feel your energies and touch your essential beings.

Freeze.

Script	I think it essential that we counterpoint the dramatic tension with a touch of Brechtian alienation . . . I want a Boalistic realism, an almost Shavian undertone to complement the socialist naivety.
Narrator	On Sunday . . .
Script	We need to overplay to exploit a Checkovian subtlety.
Narrator	*(firmly)* On Sunday, the minister returned.

Enter minister.

She has to push her way through the script group who are still discussing.

Minister	Now, let's have a look at your work. Script group first.
Script	Er, just a minute, we're still learning our lines.
Minister	Very well. Dance group – the seed that fell on good soil.

The dance group perform their piece. It should be brief and not a great deal different from their previous offering.

Minister	Very good, you're in the service. Oh, and do come to my barbeque, sing song, church grass-cutting and pew-polishing party on Saturday. Now, script group – are you ready.
Script	Please, we're just getting into character.

Minister	Very well! Improvisation, show us the seed that the birds ate.

The improvisation group perform their piece. They move into position and hold this then suddenly burst out into bird impressions with much arm waving and screeching.

Minister	Very good, you're in the service.

The improvisation group look expectantly at the minister.

Minister	Yes, yes . . . see you Saturday. Now, ARE YOU READY!
Script	We think so.
Minister	Well . . .

The script group move forward.

Script	Ahem . . . The seed that fell among thistles by the Church Scripted Drama Group. Make up by Doris, properties by Gerald. Gaffer, Jim, Key Grip, Elizabeth, Casting Director . . .
Minister	Could we just get on with it?
Narrator	Please . . .

The script group take their position. They stand with heads bowed. After too long a pause one group member looks up and says,

Script	Dead plants.
Minister	Is that it?
Script	Yes, it's bleak isn't it?
Minister	Certainly, yes.
Script	No fancy lah-de-dah stuff for us. We knew you wouldn't like it.
Narrator	The minister didn't like it and gave the script group's theme to the others.

The others move forward and throttle the script group who die noisily.

Narrator	To him who has, will more be given.

All freeze.

Moving Intercession *by Ronni Lamont*

Introduction

The theme of prayer, of communication between God and his people, is of fundamental importance in the Bible. Prayer is demanded in both the Old and New Testaments: "Turn to the LORD and pray to him, now that he is near". (Isaiah 55.6). "Be persistent in prayer, and keep alert as you pray, giving thanks to God." (Colossians 4.2).

Prayer is seen as all-pervading, touching every aspect of our lives. It is to be used in praise of God, in thanksgiving, and in asking God to be involved in change in our lives and in the lives of others. Prayer is valued as private and personal, between the individual and God, but it is also regarded as a public, shared activity on a number of occasions: "Then, in the presence of the people, Solomon went and stood in front of the altar and raised his arms in prayer." (2 Chronicles 6.12). "But when our time with them was over, we left and went on our way. All of them, together with their wives and children, went with us out of the city to the beach, where we all knelt and prayed." (Acts 21.5).

This presentation is concerned with public prayer and in particular with intercession – asking God to intervene in our world. As in the Bible references above, it uses movement and gesture as well as words, and in common with the Bible's whole message concerning prayer, the presentation recognizes that prayer requires action. The verse quoted from Isaiah 55 is immediately followed by, "Let the wicked leave their way of life and change their way of thinking." (Isaiah 55.7).

The most famous prayer in the whole Bible is followed by, "If you forgive others the wrongs they have done to you, your Father in heaven will also forgive you. But if you do not forgive others, then your Father will not forgive you the wrongs you have done." (Matthew 6.14–15).

Bible basis

■ The Bible basis for the piece is 1 Timothy 2.1–7.

The passage offers an exhortation to prayer, linking this to Christ's giving of himself" to redeem all mankind". However, as indicated above, prayer is a theme of importance throughout the whole Bible and you could find many passages to explore and discuss as you think about this presentation.

Production notes

This is a different kind of presentation because it is not in script form, but follows a pattern of activities which your group work on to produce their own interpretation of the piece. That's important because, as you'll see as you begin to work, the prayers need to be your own, prepared for your own worship in the way that suits your church best.

Useful exercises

This piece is best suited to a group with some experience. We particularly suggest that you attempt it after working through the frameworks on tension and still image. The two still-image games in the *Games and Exercises* framework may also be useful.

In terms of the group's understanding, we also suggest some sort of discussion or research into what the Bible says about prayer as a task before working on this piece.

Moving Intercession

1. Pictures of what we're praying for

Begin the creative part of the session by reading through 1 Timothy 2.1–7. Explain that you are going to use this passage as the basis of a drama that is both useful to the participants in helping them to pray, and useful to observers in helping them to focus their own prayers. Split the group into small groups. Ideally you need five groups, although you can get away with four. We suggest that about four people per group is best; three is minimum, six maximum.

Allocate to each group the presentation of one of the sections of the prayers. The list of prayers might include:

- The church
- The world
- Ourselves
- Family and friends
- Those who are sick
- Those who have died
- The life to come

Each group is to work out a still image that represents the area to be prayed for. The groups must also work out how they are going to move from a "relaxed" position into their image. To take an example, the first group (the church), may choose to present a problem relevant to your church; some stumbling block, such as the need to reach out to the local children, or a problem within the fellowship over styles of worship – you will know the type of thing for your own church!

Do remember, though, that you're not using drama here to uphold or challenge a particular point of view, but more as a "way in" for all to be involved in praying. That doesn't mean that you avoid difficult issues, but that you offer them to God and congregation in a way that is open and accessible to all, rather than in a closed and one-sided fashion. At this stage the groups only portray the problem, issue, or question, not the healing. This means that the whole thing may not be too careful at this point.

Once the groups have worked out their pictures, show them to each other. Ask for honest criticism after each one. You'll find that people think that the simplest ones are the most powerful, and they may wish to re-work their pieces. You do not have to stick rigidly to still image; groups may choose to add simple movement or sound. One possibility here is to use your group's Bible research to find appropriate words from scripture to add to their images. These can be spoken by an individual or chorally.

2. Running the pictures together

Give the groups time to set the re-worked sequences. While they are doing this, work out a ground plan of where you are going to place the groups within the performing space. To do this, you will need to take into account the order in which the groups will perform, the finishing positions (if a group finishes with everyone standing up, will they block another group?), and the need to create a balanced total image within the performing space.

See the re-worked pieces, then place the groups in their allocated spot on the floor. Explain that the action has to run pretty continuously, so as the first group finishes they need to freeze, and the second group begin.

3. The cross

You have now completed the most difficult part of the piece. Well done! We now go on to a section in which these questions and problems are offered to God in prayer. We'll use the image of the cross to represent God's involvement in our world and its needs. Get the groups to return to their original finishing positions, and to number themselves one to four/five or however many within the group. So you now have four or five number ones, (one from each group) four or five number twos, etc. The next thing to do is to work out as a group how you're all going to make the cross with your bodies. This needs to be with the arms of the cross going across the performing area and the longer part of the cross stretching from downstage to upstage.

```
         *
    *********
         *
         *
         *
```

Downstage (Audience)

You will probably want most people standing, but do experiment to see what effect can be gained by having the downstage people kneeling with the cross going up to the upstage people who are standing. Once you've organized the shape, make sure that everyone has it fixed in their minds. Emphatically explain that everyone must go to the same place in relation to everyone else every time.

We suggest the use of music to accompany the simple movement which follows, but as always do feel free to experiment – would silence be stronger at this point? If you do use music, choose a piece that suggests a controlled power. The music that we use for this piece of simple movement is called *Survival*, from the album *I can see your house from here* by Camel. It is extremely short, but very powerful. What you are looking for is a short, classical-style piece that is solemn but uplifting, and of course it's best if you find your own piece that works well for you and your group. You might think about using the church music group or a solo player for this piece. Working with music is an art in itself, so don't be afraid to spend some time on getting the timing and cues right.

The process for making the cross is simple. The number ones walk slowly from their end position to a spot on the floor. This is their position in the cross. Once the number ones have arrived, the number twos move to their positions, then the number threes, and so on. They need to carry with them the mood of their prayer as they move.

Practise moving into the cross without music a couple of times. You may need to re-arrange the cross so that it looks right, and you need to make sure that a fairly tall person stands right at the top, so that everyone can see them.

4. The contraction

The next move represents the pain of the prayer pieces that we have shared. Once the cross has been made, everyone does a simple move that is called a contraction. A contraction is what you do instinctively when someone kicks you in the stomach and winds you, but here we will slow down the movement. It can start in the middle abdomen as a tensing of muscles that will curl you in around your tummy, and the tension spreads outwards. It may take the individual right down onto the floor, it may end with them standing upright, but curled in a very "closed" position. The contraction starts once the last person to move has arrived at the cross. Hold this contracted position for a few seconds before moving on.

5. New life

As the music fades, the group turn and greet each other. There should be a sense of involvement. It's not that all problems are suddenly solved, but you do want to present a clear picture of the need to love one another if we are to begin to work with God for the answering of our prayers.

And that's the end. How you leave the performing area is up to you to work out in the way that best fits your congregation and the geography of your performing space. You may wish to involve the rest of the congregation by taking the greeting out to them, or you may choose to use a freeze to mark a clear end to the piece. It really is up to you.

Adding words

What follows is a simple plan of the piece with suggestions for readings to add context and clarity. As with all suggestions, feel free to adapt to your own tradition and forms of prayer.

1. Reader	(*Reading from the first letter to Timothy*) First of all, then, I urge that petitions, prayers, requests, and thanksgiving be offered to God for all people.
	Still images of what we are praying for. Reader prefaces each with,
2. Reader	Let us pray for, . . . the church . . . the world . . . ourselves, our family and friends . . . those who have died and the life to come.
3. Reader	For there is one God, and there is one who brings God and mankind together, the man Christ Jesus, who gave himself to redeem all mankind.
Music.	*Forming of the cross.*
4. Contraction	
5. New life	*Greetings. Music fades.*

This is a flexible piece. We used it as the basis for a workshop at a Greenbelt festival and were just into the session when the power failed – leaving us with no music! We found that we could adapt the session to fit our particular (emergency) needs, and hope that you find it useful and adaptable for use with your group.

5. Dramatic tension – framework

This can mean lots of different things to different people, but perhaps it would be true to say that it is most notable when absent. In it's simplest form it is the "suspense" that keeps an audience interested in a piece of drama. When one considers the familiarity of so much biblical material, this tension aquires a greater significance and takes more thought to achieve. Many people know that the lost son will be welcomed home, or that Samson will pull down the pillars of the building, so this framework deals with maintaining audience involvement and interest.

There are many ways of building tension into a dramatic situation and it is important to see it as a "building in" rather than an adding on. It's all about discovering the tension already in the passage, script, or situation, and finding ways of revealing this in your drama. An understanding of dramatic tension should be part of your group's working life. We can't promise instant learning, but we can share some ideas for you to consider. Remember, what follows is only by way of example, and you must use what works for you. The important thing is to have a go, give the ideas a chance to work in practice, and then develop your own ideas from there.

Getting started

Your group is gathered together for a "devising session" to create a brand new sketch based on James chapter two! Why James 2? Well, we said that this was by way of example; if the working method can produce something from this passage, you should be able to see its application to all sorts of material. Take a look at the first four verses:

> My brothers, as believers in our Lord Jesus Christ, the Lord of glory, you must never treat people in different ways according to their outward appearance. Suppose a rich man wearing a gold ring and fine clothes comes to your meeting, and a poor man in ragged

clothes also comes. If you show more respect to the well-dressed man and say to him, "Have this best seat here," but say to the poor man, "Stand over there, or sit here on the floor by my feet," then you are guilty of creating distinctions among yourselves and of making judgements based on evil motives.

(James 2.1–4)

As a group (or in smaller groups if there are enough of you), have a brainstorming session on what you see as the possible moments of tension related to the situation as described by James. You're not making up stories or creating little dramas, just getting together a few immediate reactions related to the tensions within the passage. It will be a good idea if someone jots down people's thoughts as they express them. Don't block ideas by agreeing or disagreeing, just take everything down as it comes. You might end up with a list like this:

■ Tension created by James telling his readers what they must do – some of the readers may not like this.
■ The rich man might create a tension by just walking into the meeting; all eyes would be upon him because of his fine clothes, and perhaps his manner.
■ There would be a clear tension between the appearance of the rich and poor people in the meeting.
■ A strong tension would be created between the speaker in the passage and those who feel, as James does, that Christians should not create distinctions based on wealth and appearance.

You've got some ideas together, now it's time to put them on their feet and work on them. The ideas will shape up a lot quicker than if you all sat and discussed them for another ten minutes (or two hours!). By way of example, let's concentrate on the last idea above. Go straight on to creating a piece of drama based around that tension.

Make a picture

Get the group (or in smaller groups if enough) to create a still image of the moment when the speaker invites the rich man to the place of prominence (for more on still images, see the framework on still images). Try to create an image which conveys the central tension that you have identified.

When you come to look at the images created, make sure that you comment on the other people in the scene as much as on the central characters. How does everyone else feel about this? In what way do their reactions contribute to the central tension?

Talk to the characters

Now, in order to build on and add to your group's understanding of the situation, talk to the various characters involved, after the incident. Each group member becomes a character from the passage. Possible characters might be, the rich person (man or woman, or try one of each!); the rich person's servant; the speaker (as identified by James in the passage); and other members of the meeting (you can let your imaginations go dreaming up what sort of people these might be).

After giving the group time to think about who they'll be, interview each character with the rest of the group asking questions as themselves (out of role). Again, go for a focus on the tension of the situation as revealed through the different characters' attitudes. This "talking to characters" is called hot-seating and you can find out a lot more about the various hot-seating strategies in the *Character framework*. It might be useful to read through that section before having a go at these strategies.

Try a scene

Don't talk for too long, go straight into a short improvisation. To do this, get the group to quickly prepare a version of the scene which contains the bare bones of the situation. Go back to the refined version of your still image and remind everyone of the reactions that you carefully worked on for everyone in the scene. Build this understanding into your improvisation. Stop often and talk about what you've got, gradually developing a scene which brings the passage to life in a believable way.

Add thoughts

Now try this as a way of moving things on. Replay the scene with the director stopping the action and calling on individual characters to give their thoughts.

So, the scene starts, people are coming in to the meeting. They enter at different times and in different ways. The director calls, "Freeze". The action stops. We have a still image. The director moves to a character and perhaps touches her or him on the shoulder. The character gives one thought about the present situation from their own viewpoint. Perhaps they simply say, "I've been looking forward to this all week", or "I've got something I must talk to everyone about".

The scene is restarted, perhaps by the director clicking their fingers or some such signal, and it runs until the rich person enters. Freeze again. Hear some more thoughts, and then let the scene run until the "speaker" invites the rich person to the best place and tells the poor person where they must sit. Again, hear some inner thoughts.

Stop the exercise there and remind the group that it is very important to remember that what you are aiming for is the revelation of dramatic tension. Everything else must take second place to that. With that thought in mind, continue to work at your improvisation by asking the group to play the scene with the minimum of words, with thoughts spoken by the characters saying just one word at a time. The group members will have to choose the most appropriate and telling expression of their inner thoughts. You might get something like this;

The group enters, one by one. As each person enters they give a one-word thought. You might hear words like, "Expectation", "Peaceful", "Quiet", "Anxiety", "Doubt".

The rich person enters. The action freezes. We hear three or four thoughts: perhaps "Satisfaction", "Resentment", "Dilemma", or "Respect". Then the words given in the passage are spoken. At that point stop the drama and get the group together and re-read the passage, this time going on to include verses 5-7.

> "Listen, my dear brothers! God chose the poor people of this world to be rich in faith and to possess the kingdom which he promised to those who love him. But you dishonour the poor! Who are the ones who oppress you and drag you before the judges? The rich! They are the ones who speak evil of that good name which has been given to you."
>
> (James 2.5-7)

You're now going to see if you can use what you've done so far to create a drama that puts the tension in this situation into context. After all, the tension isn't really about someone not liking someone else's style of dress! James gives us the context here. It's all about how God wants us to treat people and our attitude to riches.

Go back over what you've already done and polish it.

Remove what doesn't make for clarity. Now that you've established the idea of "one-word thoughts" you can develop it. Keep to the spirit of clarity, but allow yourself to go for short phrases, and ideas from verses 5-7, wherever they are appropriate as thoughts, such as, "Listen", "God chose the poor", "The poor are rich", "Rich in faith", and so on.

Build and work on the scene

You're working towards the end where these words from verses 5-7 will be used to contrast with what has happend in the scene. In order for that contrast to be effective it has to be in tension with what has gone before. The shape of your finished and polished improvisation could well be something like this:

■ The worshippers enter.
■ We hear some thoughts about the meeting to come.
■ The rich person enters. More thoughts.
■ The leader of the meeting invites the rich person to a place of prominence and moves the poor out of the way.
■ Thoughts build up into a crescendo using words from verses 5-7.
■ Out of the chorus of words, verses 5-7 are read, perhaps by a single voice, perhaps chorally.
■ The impact of these words freezes the action. This is the central moment of tension, so hold it. Then, out of the stillness, all turn to focus on the rich person and the speaker. Hold that image and find some telling words from the passage to end with. Perhaps, "God chose, but you dishonour."

That's one possible product of a session spent exploring this passage from a perspective of dramatic tension. Remember, all this is by way of example. It really doesn't matter if you end up with something completely different or if you apply the strategies to a different initial stimulus. The important thing is to develop your understanding of these working methods. Let's just remind ourselves of the strategies used in this framework.

Reading

■ This sounds obvious but it's basically about getting to know your source material, be it a script, Bible passage, or anything else.

Brainstorm

■ Create an atmosphere in which ideas, and feelings can flow freely. Don't approve or disapprove of people's ideas at this stage, just register and save ideas for possible later use. In this framework we used brainstorming to identify possible moments of tension.

Get on your feet

■ Not really a strategy, just a reminder to get up and try things out – don't talk for too long.

Talk to the characters

■ A useful way of moving from talk to action. Helps to fill in the background of the characters and situation.

Improvise

■ Used here to let the group try out ideas with no pressure to perform or share in a dramatic form.

Add thoughts

■ A useful way of revealing the inner tensions in a situation.

Re-read the passage

■ A reminder to go back to the source material from time to time.

Central moment of tension

■ Used here to reveal the heart of the passage and given extra dramatic impact by the use of silence.

Despite the title of this framework, dramatic tension is not really a separate, watertight approach to creating drama. It involves all other aspects of drama, from characterization to still images, and can include more theatrical features such as sound effects and lighting. It involves finding new ways of working with biblical material, and of vividly re-working familiar ideas (see *Traveller Casserole* – page 48). The following pieces, especially

I Need, I Want, are particularly receptive to the treatment suggested in this framework.

I Need, I Want *by Gordon Lamont*

Introduction

This sketch was originally written for television. *London Weekend Television* recorded a special service to celebrate the centenary of the YMCA and we were asked to contribute. Our brief was to produce a sketch of no more than three minutes portraying the state of the world, to go before a more positive section of things to celebrate and give thanks for. The state of the world in three minutes – even we wouldn't be so arrogant as to attempt it!

Bible basis

■ What we came up with grew out of the story of the rich young man as found in Matthew 19.16-30, Mark 10.17-31, and Luke 18.18-30 (although this is a strong Gospel theme and there are many other relevant passages). You might like to look at the story of the rich man and Lazarus (Luke 16.19-31) because this sketch uses a very similar structure); two people, one very wealthy, the other in great need. One has a home and a world full of things, while the other has only his clothing and begging bowl.

Production notes

This is one of those pieces that looks very stark on paper, and perhaps leaves you wondering if it's really very dramatic. Think of the whole piece in terms of the images built up in the audience's mind. As in the story of Lazarus, there should be a real contrast between the busy, "thing-filled" life of TWO and the simple, direct questioning of ONE.

Imagine an acting area that is split in two, one half is full of food, fridges, burglar alarms, etc. and the other is "full" of need. In our presentation of this sketch, we made considerable use of freezes to mark the end of sections. We held the images for just long enough to give the audience time to take them in before moving on to the next section. The natural points for these freezes seemed to us to be just before ONE announced the keyword for the next section, so TWO would freeze after, "I think I've got enough" and again after "Lettuce Spray".

We also used pauses and silences, particularly in the mimed sections at the end of the sketch. These were essential for building the tension between the relaxed and confident manner of TWO and the more desperate need of ONE. Those mimed pieces at the end are crucial to the effectiveness of the whole sketch. Take time to work on them. Each one should be no more that one simple move. Don't try to make them extra dramatic, just suggest what's going on and let the drama build inside your audience's heads.

Useful exercises

In terms of frameworks, apart from dramatic tension, you might also find some still-image material useful. We also suggest that you build some "hot-seating" into your rehearsal to develop the way that these people speak and move.

Characters

- ONE. Representing Need.
- TWO. Representing Want. Either character can be female or male.

I Need, I Want

The stage is clear. Enter ONE to downstage left, TWO to downstage right.

ONE	I need.
TWO	I want.
ONE	I need food, shelter, water, warmth.
TWO	I want . . .
ONE	Food.
TWO	Er, one of those, two of these, ten grammes of that, two kilos of this, a little of that, and a lot of this . . . how much?

During the above, TWO has been indicating his purchases.

ONE	Just a little, just enough, that's all.
TWO	I think I've got enough.

Pause.

ONE	Shelter.

TWO   Ah, burglar alarm off, and put the food away in my Scandinavian-Pine, split-level kitchenette with food processor, microwave, thermal do-dah, electric cloth wangler, double-immersion sprocket extruder, freezer, freezer bags on a roll, electric freezer bag sealer, electric freezer bag opener, electric freezer beeping noise, digital display of what beeping noise means, remote control, beeping remote control locating device, toaster, kettle, juice extractor, juice infusor, coffee grinder, organ grinder, fly spray, smell spray, cream spray, floor spray, underarm spray, breath spray, orange spray, tomato spray, [*suddenly holy*] lettuce spray.

He freezes, full of the joys of his kitchen.

Pause.

ONE   Water.

TWO moves to a shop area. He is examining what's available.

TWO   *Spring, natural, natural with bubbles, natural without bubbles, no water just bubbles, quarter litre, one litre, two litre, three. Four litre, five litre with half a litre free*

This becomes a chant which TWO continues to repeat under ONE's next speech.

ONE   Warmth. In some places where I live I am cold and I need warmth . . . in other places it's the people who are cold and they have needs as great as mine.

They come together for the first time, centre stage. ONE is now the till operator.

ONE   Ah, so that's,

ONE/   Quarter litre, one litre, two litre, three. Four litre,
TWO   five litre with half a litre free.

ONE   With half a litre free sir, that will be sir, seven pounds and ninety-nine p sir.

TWO gives ONE the money.

ONE   Thank you and shall I put the odd penny in the charity box?

73

TWO	What's the charity?
ONE	It's for food, shelter, water, and warmth.
TWO	Oh yes, of course I'm in favour of that.
ONE	So shall I put the odd penny in?
TWO	Yes, yes I want you to.
ONE	I think you mean you need me to.
TWO	No, I don't think I need anything. Good day.

Pause.

ONE	I need.
TWO	I want.
ONE	Food.

TWO mimes eating larger-than-life hamburger. ONE mimes an empty belly.

TWO	Shelter.

ONE tries to shelter from the elements. TWO switches on TV and relaxes.

ONE	Water.

TWO mimes placing a glass under the tap and taking a drink. ONE scrabbles in the ground searching for water.

TWO	Warmth

ONE hugs themself for warmth. TWO switches on an electric fire and holds his hands out to the warmth. Pause.

ONE	I need.
TWO	I need . . . nothing. I want the world.

ONE shakes their head.

ONE	I need . . . you need.

Freeze.

Saint Sharon's *by Nick Page*

Introduction

This is a reworking of the parable of the unforgiving servant and for a change all the main roles are female! In the hockey match towards the end the girls from the Florence Nightingale School could be played by males wearing suitable kit and straw boaters, brandishing cricket stumps. It is included as an example of how "slapstick" can be used to give an effective message.

Bible basis

■ Matthew 18.23-25

Production notes

The characters in this piece are more types than individuals, but study of Deirdre's motivation would be useful (see the characters framework on page 11). Much of Deirdre's character is created through her lisp and this can help comedy too. Timing is very important in arranging the hockey match, and the use of the "slow motion" in rehearsal will enable an effective choreography to be produced (see the suggestions below) and prevent broken bones.

The costume is fuller than in some other sketches, and reflects traditional public school uniforms and dress. Hockey sticks and cricket stumps (or equivalents) are required props. Music is suggested during the hockey match and any "sports" music would be appropriate ("Match of the Day" or "Chariots of Fire", for example).

Useful exercises

Quite a lot of tension can be created in this piece, so the various approaches suggested in the *Dramatic Tension* framework should help prepare it. Study of *Getting going* (page 90) and *Doing it together* (page 93) from the *Making Moves* framework will help in rehearsing the hockey match.

Saint Sharon's

To the tune of the Eton Boating Song.

ALL   Welcome to St Sharon's,
             A school of most high renown,
             Though the Health Inspector
             Is trying to close us down.
             Play up at St Sharon's!

The school where we all belong,
We'll raise our girlish voices
As one in the old school song.

The schoolbell rings. Exit all except Head and Deirdre.

HEAD   (Narrating) It is nine o'clock on a Tuesday morning and the ancient and noble school of St Sharon's is beginning another day. In her study, Miss Henrietta Water-Buffalo, the stately, much-respected head of the school has an unpleasant task to perform.

There is a knock at the door.

(As Head) Come in!

DEIRDRE   You wanted to thee me Mith Water-Buffalo?

HEAD   Indeed I do. Come in. I have here a list of complaints about your behaviour from your teachers. It makes impressive reading.

DEIRDRE   Ith thomething wrong?

HEAD   Wrong? You realize that you have failed to hand in any prep for the past . . . *(Checks list)* . . . three and a half years.

DEIRDRE   Er . . . my hamthter ate it.

HEAD   You failed to hand in any prep this morning.

DEIRDRE   I . . . er . . . I had a headache latht night.

HEAD   Did you see matron?

DEIRDRE   Yeth.

HEAD   What did she say?

DEIRDRE   Thee wanted to amputate.

HEAD   However, prep is just one of your shortcomings. The list of your misbehaviour makes Jack the Ripper look like a choirboy. You have a history of being cheeky to teachers. On prize-giving day you were found running a book on the results. And I don't know what it was you put in the music teacher's ear-trumpet but it took the skills of three highly-qualified surgeons to remove it from her ear.

DEIRDRE   Jutht a joke, you know, a bit of a wheeth.

HEAD   You have been round the school with a piece of chalk writing rude limericks on the walls, on the doors, and even on some of the less mobile teachers. You threw tomatoes at the Chaplain . . .

DEIRDRE   An ecthpretion of belief.

HEAD	It's not your job to question the eternal truths of the Church, Deirdre. That's what we have bishops for. It is your job to behave yourself. I'm afraid the time has come for me to write to your parents.
DEIRDRE	Oh no Mith, pleath no! I'll reform. I'll be good. I'll behave mythelf. Pleeath! They'll take me away and I love the old thchool, really I do!
HEAD	Mmmmmmmmmmmmmm.
DEIRDRE	I promith to be good. Croth my heart and hope to die!
HEAD	Oh very well. I will let you off this time. But in future your behaviour had better be exemplary my girl.

(Narrating) And so, with a sigh of relief, Deirdre left the Head's office and went back to her dorm.

DEIRDRE	Phew! Thurvived that one. I'd better watch my thtep.

(Enter Stephanie).

Hello. Who do I thee? Why, if it ithn't thweet, pure little Thtephanie, the Goody-Gumdropth of the Third. I hate her becauth thee'th good and kind and nice, but most of all becauth I can't say Thtephanie. *(Calls.)* Thtephanie! Oh Thtephanie!

STEPH-ANIE	Hello Deirdre, what do you want?
DEIRDRE	Jutht a little matter of thome money owed. You borrowed the money off me and I want it back.
STEPH-ANIE	Oh, but I haven't got it yet. I'll have it next week I promise.
DEIRDRE	Not good enough Thtephanie. I want it now. You signed me an IOU remember? And if you don't pay up I'll tell everybody what I know about you and the grotherth boy behind the bithycle shedth.
STEPH-ANIE	Gasp! You wouldn't be so cruel! It was a brief fling. I was a fool lured by promises of true love and free pineapples.
DEIRDRE	The money or I talk!
STEPH-ANIE	No! Take anything! Oh, the shame!
DEIRDRE	All right then . . . I'll take the thigned photo that hangth in your locker.
STEPH-ANIE	No . . . not . . . not Cliff!

DEIRDRE I'll tell . . .

STEPH- You are cruel, cruel. Take it, it's yours.
ANIE

(Exit Deirdre and Stephanie.)

HEAD *(Narrating).* And so Deirdre had her sweaty little
hands on Stephanie's most prized possession. It was
the afternoon of the great hockey match. St Sharon's
were playing their arch-rivals the Florence
Nightingale School for Young Offenders.

(Enter St Sharon's team.)

Both sides took it very seriously and the St Sharon's
team had been training for weeks. It was rumoured
that some of the Florence Nightingale team even
partook of certain artificial stimulants.

*(Enter the Florence Nightingale team. Both teams take
up positions and mime the action as described by the
Head.)*

Bully off! Stephanie plays the ball out to Doris. Doris to
Cecily and Cecily to Henrietta and Henrietta to Frank
who is tackled! And the girls of Florence Nightingale
surge forward, their beards flowing in the wind, three
passes and . . .

All Wham!

HEAD The ball is in the back of the St Sharon's net. *(As
Head).* Play up St Sharon's! Come on Stephanie!

STEPH- I'm doing my best, Head!
ANIE

(The teams freeze.)

HEAD *(Narrating).* But Stephanie seems strangely distracted
and pre-occupied, and the whole team suffers as a
result. At half-time, St Sharon's are losing 37 to nil.
(As Head). Stephanie! What's the matter girl? You are
playing like a ruptured baboon.

STEPH- I don't know Miss. I'm strangely distracted and
ANIE pre-occupied.

HEAD Come on girl, you can tell me.

STEPH-
ANIE   *(Crying).* Oh . . . oh . . . Cliff!

          (She starts to sob loudly on the Head's shoulder).

HEAD   *(Narrating).* And the young captain of the hockey team
          breaks down in the Head's arms . . . in the . . .
          (Shouting over the increasing din of Stephanie's tears) . . .
          and the whole story comes out . . . I said the whole
          story . . . Oh, shut up girl! Second half!

          *(The second half is played in slow motion backed by suitable
          music (see production notes). Stephanie runs rings around
          everybody and scores while the rest end up in a pile with
          Deirdre on top).*

DEIRDRE   I thay, how perfectly beathtly! That brat Thtephanie
          thcored thirty-eight goalth in the thecond half and
          won uth the match. Thee maketh me thick. And now
          Mith Water-Buffalo wanth to thee me again.

          (Exit Florence Nightingale team and Deirdre stands up).

HEAD   I have written to your parents Deirdre. There can be no
          place for the likes of you in my school. I sentence you
          to be taken from this place and seated in Miss
          Frimley's algebra class until dead or until your parents
          come and collect you, which ever comes first.
          (Addressing school). Girls, we must learn from this. We
          all do things we ought not. But if you are willing to try
          again, you will always find forgiveness from me. Let
          us sing the School Song.

ALL   *(Tune as before).*
          Here at St Sharon's,
          The truth is plain today,
          Forgive and be forgiven,
          Or else be sent away.
          If you're truly sorry,
          The punishment is witheld,
          But if you were lying,
          You're likely to be expelled.
          (Repeat last 4 lines of melody.)
          Play up St Sharon's
          Play up girls and fight the fight,

And from St Sharon's,
We bid you a fair goodnight.

(All exit.)

The Baker *by Nick Page*

Introduction

The aim of this piece is to show the loving message of Jesus in spite of all attempts to kill him and destroy the message. Borrowing its central image from a poem by Charles Causley, *The Baker* takes Jesus' claim to be the Bread of Life and looks at the reactions of various people to him. The rhythmic nature of the lines powerfully underlines the movement and action portrayed in the presentation. It needs to be slickly performed, is ideal for evangelistic purposes, and could also be used in street theatre. It enables attention to be drawn to the figure of Christ in a new way. Another piece which views the rejection of Jesus is *No Room* (page 84).

Bible basis

■ This sketch explores a number of biblical areas, particularly John 6.33-51 – Jesus as the Bread of Life.

Other areas which might help in approaching this piece are:

■ Matthew 26.1-5; 27.11-26 – Opposition to Jesus
■ Luke 23.26-48 – Crucifixion
■ Mark 16.1-20 – The resurrection

Production notes

Portraying Christ on stage needs careful thought and can be a challenging and disturbing experience. The actor playing the Baker needs to be aware of this and sensitive to the role itself and to the audience.

The piece is written with five players in mind. The Baker, One, and Two are male voices, and Three and Four are female, but any combination is possible. More than five players may clutter the stage and prove difficult to arrange with movement. It is important that the flow and rhythms of the verse are maintained and therefore the movement must be well rehearsed.

The degree of realism for costume is of secondary importance but it would be useful to give a distinction between the Baker and the rest (e.g. a different coloured costume or apron).

Useful exercises

■ The exercise in the *Making moves* framework could help in producing the movement.
■ In rehearsal exercises such as *Talk to the characters*, (page 67) and *Add thoughts* (page 67) will help the actors understand the motivation of the characters.

The Baker

One He entered the city on Sunday
    All the people gathered to see,
    For they said that he baked the best bread in the world
    And he gave it to people for free.

    (By now One, Two, Three, and Four are on stage in a line with One CSL. During the next verse Baker crosses in front of them from SR to SL).

    But he didn't look much like a baker
    There was something unreal in this eyes,
    And the people who wanted to see him
    Went quiet as he passed them by.

    (Baker stands DSL. The others huddle together as if gossiping DSR).

Two He comes from a northerly village they said
One
Two And I have heard tell
    That his father was not his real father,
    That his mother was not a good girl.

    (One, Two, and Four become scribes as Three crosses SL and Baker approaches them.)

Three On the Monday he went to the Temple
    To offer his bread to the scribes
Baker Take and eat it,

Three	He told them,
Baker	For mine is the bread that saves lives.
Three	The scribes said,
One	
Two	No thank you.
Four	
Four	We'd rather

Not eat if you really don't mind.
I'm sure there are others more hungry than us,

One	The lepers
Two	The sick,
Four	or the blind.

(The Baker turns and crosses to Three; One and Four follow on and receive the bread he hands out during the next verse.)

Two   On the Tuesday the Baker went walking
And he gave out his bread to the poor.
He offered his bread to the taxman,
He offered his bread to the whore.
He said,

Baker   My bread is baked by my father
And those who will taste it will see
That the bread baked on this world is stale,
Only my bread can set someone free.

(One joins Two DSR. As the Baker feeds Three and Four USL.)

Four   On Wednesday the rest of the bakers
Watched the people flock to him in droves.
Their leader said,

One   We must do something,
Nobody's buying our loaves.
I think I know someone who's willing
To hand the man over to me.
I'll see if he's open to offers,
Thirty pieces, I think, is his fee.

(Two marches CS and as Baker offers him bread, arrests him.)

Three   They arrested the Baker on Thursday
And charged him with all that they could.

(The Baker appeals to Three and Four who turn away. He is then thrown to the floor and One roughly picks him up to present him to Two, who is now the Chief of Police.)

They turned all the people against him
And claimed that his bread was no good.
They took him before the Chief of Police
Who couldn't quite understand
The need for this sudden trial
Of this curious baker man.

(Three and Four huddle conspiritorially DSL.)

Four	But the scribes and the breadmen united

Four   But the scribes and the breadmen united
For on two things they both could agree;
That people could not live forever
And you shouldn't give bread out for free.
The policeman looked up at the Baker.
He said,

Two   I'm just doing my job.

Four   Then he washed his hands in a basin
And he handed him out to the mob.

(One throws Baker across stage.)

One   So the Baker was taken and beaten.
For his clothing the soldiers drew lots.
And at nine in the morning on Friday
They nailed him up on the cross.

(The Baker is crucified in silence. During the next verse he crouches down UCS as the others move around in mourning).

Three   His friends took him down six hours later.
He had died and the light had grown dim.
They folded his body like paper,
And they wiped all the blood from his skin.

Four   They borrowed a tomb for his burial
And they all thought the story complete.
On Saturday nobody smiled much,
And nobody wanted to eat.

One   But on Sunday morning some women
Went to attend to the dead,
But when they arrived at the tomb all they found
Was the smell of new baked bread!

(The Baker jumps up and the others turn to meet him.)

Two   He had burst from the tomb and had risen
And his smile was like showers of rain.
He said to his friends,

Baker   Go and tell all the world
The Baker is baking again.
I will be with you forever
For I have returned from the dead

(The Baker leads everybody back out through the audience.)

I have enough to feed all of mankind,
I am the new baked bread.

No Room *by Derek Haylock*

Introduction

There are links between this presentation and *The Baker* (page 80). Its aim is to show that Jesus is rejected by many today as he was in Bethlehem two thousand years ago. It is an entirely serious piece of mime designed for a Christmas service. The familiar theme of there being no room for Jesus in Bethlehem is taken as a starting point, and the sketch highlights the fact that he was rejected during his lifetime, to the point of crucifixion. It continues by showing that in some ways little has changed today. The text is taken entirely from the Bible.

The tension in the piece comes through the actions rather than the narration, and through the visual impact of the events with their stark contrasts.

Bible basis

■ Luke 2.4-7; John 1.10-11; Isaiah 53.3,7; 1 Peter 2.4.

Production notes

Only the reader has any spoken lines in this sketch and the lines could be pre-recorded or spoken offstage. There are nine citizens and Mary, Joseph, and Jesus. Events and actions rather than exploration of the character are the focus here, and Jesus, gentle and loving, forms the dramatic centre of that action. The stage is empty except for a ramp (or steps) which leads to a raised platform at the back centre of the stage.

Costume could reflect the traditional Christmas story treatment or could move away from historical costume to give the piece a more symbolic or modern approach, using modern clothes. As with *The Baker* (page 80) some distinguishing costume for Jesus might be useful, or the group might want to show how he identifies with ordinary people.

Music forms an important background to the piece. Seasonal music and carols (pre-recorded) could form an effective contrast with the events on stage. Silences at dramatic points (e.g. the crucifixion) are vital to achieve the appropriate effect. Sound effects of traffic and modern life can also be pre-recorded for the final part of the sketch. The only essential props are the nine placards with B, E, T, H, L, E, H, E, or M, on one side and "sorry" or "full up" signs on the other.

Useful Exercises

See the note on *Adding thoughts* (page 67) or *Talk to the characters* (page 67) from the *Tension* framework. Concentration is a particularly important aspect of mime, so the concentration-building games and exercises might form a basis to improve this.

No Room

> (*The nine citizens march on slowly, forming a straight line across the centre of the stage. They are carrying placards, which when they turn to face the audience, will be seen to spell out B E T H L E H E M. Mary and Joseph enter*).

Reader Joseph went from the town of Nazareth in Galilee to the town of Bethlehem in Judaea, the birthplace of King David.

> (*Citizens turn to face the audience.*)

Reader He went to register with Mary, who was promised in marriage to him. She was pregnant, and while they were in Bethlehem the time came for her to have her baby.
> There was no room for them to stay in the inn.

> (*Music up.*)

(The citizen on the extreme right of the line takes one pace to the right, thus making a gap in the line. Mary and Joseph head towards this gap, but as they reach it the next citizen takes a pace to the right and closes it. This then opens up a new gap in the line. But this too is closed by the next citizen.

As Mary and Joseph make their way along the line, each gap that opens is closed in front of them. As each citizen moves they turn their placard round to reveal messages such as "NO ROOM", "SORRY", "FULL UP", "NO VACANCIES", "TRY ELSEWHERE", on the reverse side. Finally, Mary and Joseph walk away and exit).

(Music down.)

Reader   **She gave birth to her first son, wrapped him in strips of cloth, and laid him in a manger — there was no room for them to stay in the inn.**

(Music up.)

(Citizens kneel and lower their placards. Jesus enters and stands behind the kneeling citizens, who have their backs to him.)

(Music down.)

Reader   **The Word was in the world, and though God made the world through him, yet the world did not recognize him. He came to his own country but his own people did not receive him.**

(Music up.)

(Citizens stand. Face Jesus. Then turn their backs on him. During the following reading they walk slowly backwards, pushing him up the ramp. Finally he reaches the platform and stands there above the crowd. He turns to face away from the audience).

Reader   **We despised him and rejected him; he endured suffering and pain. He was treated harshly, but endured it humbly; he never said a word. Like a lamb about to be slaughtered, like a sheep about to be sheared, he never said a word.**
They crucified him.

(Jesus snaps into a crucified posture. Silence. After a few seconds the citizens walk off slowly. Then Jesus turns and walks down the ramp to a position centre stage.)

Reader   **Come to the Lord, the living stone rejected by man as worthless, but chosen by God as valuable.**

(Jesus raises his hands in invitation.)

(Modern-day sound effects are heard: e.g. traffic noise, cash register, pop music, television advertisements, computer bleeps. The citizens march on again, rather more quickly. They busy themselves with various things, such as reading the Radio Times, listening to a cassette player, shopping, football, etc.

The stage is full of activity with the crowd ignoring Jesus. Gradually they crowd round him, still ignoring him, and push him out. He falls out of the crowd, forward onto the stage. As this happens there is a dramatic, loud drumbeat, the crowd freezes, and there is silence. Jesus slowly picks himself up from the floor.

He looks sadly behind him at the crowd. Then slowly and deliberately he turns and looks round the audience. Then, lowering his head, he walks solemnly down the centre aisle, and exits from the building.)

6. Making moves: Choreography framework

Your group will be using movement quite extensively already. Even if you only ever do radio plays, you'll have built up quite an understanding of the importance of a sense of movement as different characters come in and out of "sound focus". If you're actuallly seen as you act, then your notions of the power of movement and stillness as ways of communicating thought and feeling will be highly developed. This framework is all about exploring and, most importantly, realizing the facts. If you've approached the idea of thinking and planning in terms of movement rather than words with some trepidation, then it's time to realize that movement is as natural to drama as it is to life.

This sense of movement at the heart of things is clear in the Bible:

> In the beginning, when God created the universe, the earth was formless and desolate. The raging ocean that covered everything was engulfed in total darkness, and the power of God was moving over the water. Then God commanded, "Let there be light – then the light appeared. Then he separated the light from the darkness, and he named the light "Day" and the darkness "Night".
>
> Genesis 1.1-5

A very dramatic picture, and one which it is impossible to visualize without a strong sense of movement – we "see" a raging ocean, the power of God is seen moving over the water, and God separates the light from the dark. This rich sense of movement is esen throughout the Bible, in the acts of the prophets, the poetry of the psalms, in the healings and miracles of Jesus, in the parables, and perhaps most powerfully, in the resurrection. God has made us to inhabit a physical world, given us bodies with which to enjoy that world and with which to express our love and joy, and our questions, doubts, and even our anger towards him. This is why movement is central to life and therefore to drama. To use movement properly we need to think about how and why we make moves.

Getting started

In this framework we will attempt to give some pointers for how to set about choreographing (if you prefer, use the word "planning") a piece of movement to pre-recorded music. A good example of this type of piece is *Endpeace*, which you can find on page 109. If you're not yet ready for a "movement-only" piece, then simply take what is useful for what you are working on – say the end of the dramatic tension framework. Above all, use our scribblings as a framework on which to build and develop your own ideas and working methods.

One good way to prepare for planning movement is to take yourself and your group to see as many other groups as possible. Go and watch local or fringe dance groups and see what they are doing; national companies if you can afford them; and mime artists – as well as looking at straight plays with a "movement eye".

You will find that experiencing the work of others stretches your ideas and helps to develop your critical faculties. Watch carefully, one performer at a time, and see exactly what they are doing. You might also join a contemporary dance class, an aerobics class, a jazz-dance class, anything that will make your body do different things to what you normally ask it to do. And don't get daunted by all those willowy females in glamorous leotards. You'll soon be as supple as they if you stick at it.

Think movement

We've suggested at the head of this framework that the Bible can be seen very much as movement orientated, so why not try a Bible study where you think about the movement in the passage? Here are some movement-based questions drawn from Luke's account of the arrest and trial of Jesus.

- Why did Jesus withdraw "about a stone's throw" from the disciples at the Mount of Olives?
- Why did he, why does anyone, kneel to pray?
- What sort of movement picture is suggested by the words, "Father, if you will, take this cup of suffering away from me"?
- How might Jesus' fervour in prayer have expressed itself in

movement?

A few simple questions like these can help to bring a passage into focus in a new way. Of course, you can actually make the pictures as well as talk about them, and this would be an excellent way in to working on a movement piece based on such a passage.

Planning

You've a session coming up and you need to be ready with some movement ideas. How? Getting an idea on the go occurs in different ways to different people.

We tend to start with the music, but finding inspiring music that's different from your last dance can be difficult, so it's a good idea to get into the habit of listening across as wide a range as you can. The alternative to simply letting a piece of music inspire you (and the one that is more likely to occur in a church-based group) is that someone will ask you to produce a piece, and the group will decide that perhaps this is the big one, and it's time to go for movement.

Choosing the music

These are the criteria that we would apply when trying to find a suitable piece of music:

- Does it make you want to move? If it doesn't, scrap it.
- If it has words, do they fit the theme if they are audible?
- Is the music reasonably accessible to the audience, or will they mentally turn off?
- Is it short enough? Nothing is worse than a long-winded piece of dance that was made because the director liked the music but couldn't fill it all.

When you have found a piece that fulfils all the above, come and tell us so that we can use it! Clearly, you will have to compromise, but try and find the best piece for fulfilling as many criteria as you can.

Getting going

Listen to that music as much as you can for a week at least before you start. In the car, on the personal stereo, feeding the baby in the middle of the night, when the neighbours come round to complain about the noise in the night! You have to know every bar, word, and change of rhythm if you are to make this piece work. You are going to have to walk into the first rehearsal with enough ideas at your memory tips to give your group confidence, particularly if this is all new to them – you must provide a secure framework within which to work and that means knowing the music. Don't be too daunted by this. If you're using Rock or Pop music you'll find that many tracks have a chorus, and it's usually worth working out what you want to happen in the chorus first of all. There are a few points to note about this.

■ You can use a chorus to give a central focus to your piece – make it the heart of the story or message of the dance.
■ You'll find that you've worked out a lot of the piece very quickly because the chorus repeats.
■ It can be very annoying if you work out a brilliant bit for part of a verse, only to discover that everyone is then in the wrong place for the chorus you worked out so painstakingly! Don't forget, if the chorus occurs several times it's nice to put in some variety for your audience after the first couple of times – it keeps them awake and can be a useful way of stressing a point.

Find a space in which to try out ideas . We use our sitting room so you can't have that – find your own space. It really doesn't need to be that big at this stage. Work out a part at a time and try to keep a sort of floor plan in your mind, so folk don't collide. You might find it useful to jot down your thoughts as you go along. As you work, bear in mind the following points.

■ Keep it simple if this is your first go. If you have lots of different movements going on at the same time, you might soon run out of varied ideas. People can't watch more than one small area of stage at the same time – it could be a waste to have too much going on unless that's the effect you are aiming for.
■ Keep the central theme or story in mind at all times. Cut out anything that obscures what you want the piece to be about.
■ Don't let the moves be too fast in terms of the speed the dancers are moving at – bad dance looks worse speeded up. Slow strong moves look good even if they are incredibly simple.
■ Don't wander off the track because you fancy some clever moves that you learnt at your class last week. File these mentally until the right piece comes along.

■ Consider the piece from different perspectives. Look at what you've got from the point of view of its floor pattern, then think about it in terms of different types of movement used and the different speeds of movement. A friend once reminded us that a piece of dance needs "Pauses – like a sentence needs commas and a full stop".

■ Use still pictures to emphasize the point, and to let this brilliant visual image that you have created sink in to your audience's memory.

■ In the same way that teachers, preachers, and the like repeat the most important phrases so that you remember them, repeat important pieces of dance; then repeat them again, with slight variations if appropriate.

Making an entrance

Think about how your dancers are going to come on; do they start on stage, frozen, or are they off stage at the start? Do they come on in groups? Singly? At what speed? Do they walk into position and then freeze, or do they keep going once they are on?

This is the most important section of the dance for both the group and the audience. For the group because if they can do it and it feels good, you've gone a long way towards gaining their commitment to the piece. For the audience because if they don't like the beginning, you've got a big job on getting them "hooked" and involved.

Moving on

If you were clever, you used up far more music than you imagined possible in just getting the thing started, and you're probably into your chorus already – wasn't that bad, was it? Don't forget, if you do your planning in a small space, it'll take longer in the larger space you are going to perform in. If you have picked a short piece of music, you can probably put this book down now and carry on, feeling wonderfully inspired and very clever. If, however, you've still got fifteen minutes of Mahler to plough through, you have a choice of three actions at this point:

■ Take what you have to your group, work it out, and then carry on, working with the group, having seen how that bit went down.

■ Give up and change your music!

■ Carry on, on a different day, working on your own. But show what you have done to some sympathetic person who is brave and honest enough to say if they think you have barked up the wrong tree.

Doing it together

So here you are, sitting with your group and about to start the session. Manic hysteria is rising in your throat; "What if it doesn't work? What if they don't like it? What if . . ." All we can say is it doesn't get better. If one of us has a new idea, we feel exactly the same way.

Play some games to make folk laugh and feel more at ease. Do a good warm up, then play your music, possibly all, possibly just the opening and explain what you have planned. Say that you have rough ideas for the movement, but that all contributions will be greatly accepted. Don't lord it over the group, just explain the ideas. Then play the beginning section again and get them going. You do need to direct, and stand out of it.

A few points to think about at this stage:

■ Be prepared for a person to move in a totally different way to how you saw it when you were planning the piece, and if they can't do it how you wanted, be flexible enough to accept this – it may well be a very good thing and introduce new angles and strengths.
■ Show the group what you mean as well as talking about it. You may also have to place their bodies in the positions required. Once people have been put into shape, they tend to remember it.
■ Repeat sections as and when you feel it necessary so that people remember what's happened and feel comfortable with the work rate.
■ Bear in mind that although you may feel it hard to remember all these moves – you're remembering several parts – each group member need only remember their own.
■ Make space for group members to put in ideas. Provide a "framework with holes"; the framework gives security, the holes provide creative involvement.
■ Most importantly, encourage the group. If it looks good, say so. It's quite a shock to you when, not only does it work, but it's good too! You need to express how it's going. Expect to feel protective and maternal/paternal about the piece you have

created. Movement can be intensely personal.

So, suddenly, it's almost done. A few words about the ending:

■ Is it to stop in a freeze? This is very powerful if you want the audience to remember a particular visual image. If you do, how will the group know when to move off? How will they make their exit? We have found that a simple count to five and then a quick exit that is clearly out of role works well.
■ Do they exit singly, in groups, en masse? Quickly, slowly? Choose the most appropriate for the mood and story of your piece.
■ Are you prepared for applause? Embarrassed silence? How would these affect the message of what you have just done? These details need to be thought about as your group could be easily thrown if they found themselves in a situation they had not prepared for.

As you can see, ending is as important as beginning, and can be shabbier, as you and the group are thinking, "Thank goodness that's all over." A bad end ruins what would have been a good dance.

Summary

Finally, there's been a lot of "tips" in this framework which we hope will build confidence, because for us, lack of confidence is all that seems to hold so many groups back. Use these four "watchwords" as a way of thinking about movement-based drama.

■ Confidence	You use movement already, so don't think of this as something "special" or "difficult".
■ Simplicity	The best ideas are often the simplest.
■ Planning	Careful, prayerful, planning is all important.
■ Flexibility	Allow for and adapt to the strengths and weaknesses of your group.

The Beatitudes
(Cross Purposes Drama Group)

Introduction

This piece uses short cameo actions to represent each beatitude, with a linking symbol, the cross, throughout. There is scope for devising your own ways of representing both the words and actions described in the text. The following description is as it was originally performed, with five people. We have split the text into eight sections for ease of understanding in rehearsal. When you perform the piece, the sections will merge together. There is scope to include music to accompany this piece.

Note

This piece looks complicated in written form but you will find that the basic floor pattern soon makes sense if you take time to walk through it with the right number of people and if you make sure that you really understand the terms used for positions on the acting area.

Upstage is towards the back, away from the audience.

Downstage is the front.

Left and *right* are as from the actor's point of view looking at the audience.

These terms do not mean that you can only have an audience on one side when you perform, but for clarity in understanding the text adopt one side as the audience side and make sure that everyone is clear about which it is. Please see the diagram on page x.

Bible basis

■ Matthew 5.3-12

Production notes

■ The Cross
   This is the dramatic strength of the piece, through its repitition and physical presence. It is formed with two people, standing, facing in opposite directions, shoulder to shoulder. Their near arms are upright and together, their far arms stretched out

straight in front of them. As always, do experiment with the formation of the cross to get an idea that you are happy with. These crosses form and melt using different actions throughout the piece.

■ The speaking

The piece is not narrated. In effect it is a choral piece, and it starts with everyone speaking. Each beatitude is spoken by one or two people. Feel free to experiment with who speaks and when, to create a piece that is right for your group. We have used the New International Version in this script but you may like to experiment with other versions.

Useful exercises

The following workshop activities are suggested as a way of preparing to work on the Beatitudes.

■ Read Matthew 5.3-12. Each person in the group reads a different beatitude so that all get a chance to speak and listen.
■ Ask each person to express what they think each Beatitude means in simple language and perhaps with everyday examples. Discuss the results.
■ Split into pairs. Each pair take two Beatitudes and work out a still image for each.
■ Discuss the results.
■ Add in the words and experiment with the sound texture, perhaps adding other sounds or trying different ways of saying the words.

The Beatitudes

■ Start with the five performers standing in a broad arc, facing the audience.

All five repeat the word "Blessed" five times, getting gradually louder while the following movement takes place:

1 and *2* form a cross upstage centre. *3* and *4* kneel in front of it.

5 walks downstage right and completes the saying of the first Beatitude,

5.   "Blessed are the poor in spirit *(pause)* . . . for theirs is the Kingdom of Heaven".

■ The cross dissolves, 1 and 2 raising the two kneelers, who in turn form a new cross. Of the two who formed the old cross, 1 moves upstage right, while 2 moves downstage left and kneels, representing the mourner.

1.   "Blessed are those who mourn . . . "

Part of the cross (3) moves to comfort the mourner; the other part of the cross (4) kneels.

1.   " . . . for they will be comforted."

■ 2 and 3 now form a new cross downstage left. 1 moves arrogantly from upstage right passing behind 4. They approach the cross and attempt to pull it apart – the cross stays firm. The action leaves 1 frozen in a still image.

5.   "Blessed are the meek . . . "

The cross dissolves and 3 pushes the arrogant 1 to a low, crushed position while 4 rises and moves to join 2 in a new cross.

5.   " . . . for they will inherit the earth."

■ 5 approaches 1 and attempts to raise her, using 3 as an anchor.

4.   "Blessed are those who hunger and thirst for righteousness . . . "
2.   " . . . for they will be filled."

As 2 speaks, 5 and 1 form a new cross as the cross formed by 4 and 2 dissolves.

■ 4 and 2 now begin a mimed battle as in a hand-to-hand fight using simple weapons. They use the whole stage ending downstage centre. As 4 is about to deliver the final blow, they pause and then throw their weapon away. During this, 3 has moved round the back of the action, speaking the following lines.

3.   "Blessed are the merciful . . . "

4 forms a new cross with 1 as 5 moves away to upstage right.

3.   " . . . for they will be shown mercy."

You will now have a cross (4 and 1)which is downstage left with 5 diagonally opposite at upstage right. 2 and 3 now move to stand between the cross and 5. 5 approaches the cross, slowly and deliberately.

---

2.   "Blessed are the pure in heart . . . "

2 and 3 attempt to entice 5 from their course, but 5 continues through them. 2 and 3 freeze in their enticing positions.

3.   " . . . for they will see God."

5 forms a new cross with 4.

---

2 and 3 form a new image of rejection of each other.

1.   "Blessed are the peacemakers . . . "

2 and 3's image melts to form a new cross, upstage centre.

5.   " . . . for they shall be called sons of God."

5 and 4 move slowly towards 1. They grab them roughly, drag them to upstage centre, and nail them to the cross. The hammer blows should coincide with "persecuted" in the following words,

2.   "Blessed are those who are"
ALL   "Persecuted, PERSECUTED, PERSECUTED"

| 2. | "Because of righteousness . . . " |
| 3. | " . . . for theirs is the Kingdom of Heaven." |

---

5 and 4 stand either side of the cross and victim. They will now be back in their original position in the arc. 2 and 3 take the "dead" 1 and lower them to the floor. They kneel to form an arch which "entombs" the curled up body.

| 5. | "Blessed are you . . . " |
| 4. | " . . . when people insult you . . . " |

2 stands and resumes their original place in the arc.

| 2. | "And persecute you . . . " |

3 stands and resumes their original place in the arc.

| 3. | "And say all kinds of evil things against you." |

1 stands and resumes their original place in the arc.

| 1. | "Because of me." |
| ALL | "Rejoice and be glad, for great is your reward in Heaven, HEAVEN, HEAVEN, HEAVEN." |

The "Heaven's" get progressively louder and on the final shout the outer arms should be thrown upwards while everyone looks up.

Rubble Blues *by Frank McGregor*

Introduction

The idea for this piece came out of a Bible study on Nehemiah! As its name suggests, it is a blues song sung by a chorus (and actors in places) while the actors mime the actions related. It has been included here because it gives straightforward movement instructions within a framework which should be reasonably easy to follow. The Good News Bible version of Nehemiah contains so many rhymes that the first half of the song almost literally wrote itself!

Like many Top 20 hit records, parts of *Rubble Blues* were

written while the author was travelling across London on the Tube, and the message of the piece is that whatever the obstacles and opposition, obedience to God's instructions will lead to eventual success.

Bible basis

- Nehemiah 1 – 7

Production notes

Music

Rubble Blues is loosely based around an eight-bar blues sequence in the key of A. The melody for verse one has been split into two parts, a) and b). Each part is eight bars long and acts as a basic melody guide for the other verses where symbols a) and b) appear. If you have difficulty with the music then the piece can be performed entirely as a dramatic poem, perhaps with a sung chorus and guitar accompaniment.

Character

The main character, Nehemiah, has a determination and a humanity which helps to create his relationship with the audience, and he carries much of the action. The link between the various elements (words, music, and action) is obviously crucial, and this is where a significant amount of rehearsal will need to be concentrated. It is probably better to get the music and singing together first, and then work on the mime.

Cast

- Nehemiah
- Hanani
- King
- Sanballat
- Tobiah
- Geshem
- Donkey
- Soldiers
- Builders
- Choir

As *Rubble Blues* has a "cast of thousands" some doubling up of parts will be necessary.

Props

All the props may be mimed, but the use of some simple props and costume can help distinguish characters and emphasize the

The Rubble Blues
Frank McGregor

arr. C. Norton

effects. Some items you might consider are:

- Butler's cloth
- King's crown
- Scrolls
- Donkey ears and hooves

Useful exercises

Large gestures and clear expressions are essential to the mimed actions, and will help create humour in the piece. Group involvement and co-operation can be aided by trying some of the exercises suggested in the *Games* framework (*Instant Animals* or *Following Bodies* for example – page 4). Some research (reading or discussion) might help the group understand the context and the issues involved.

See the *Research* section in the *Character* framework (page 16). Finally, read or re-read the advice in *Making moves – Doing it together* (page 93).

Rubble Blues is available on audio tape from the author, c/o:

1 Millbrook Road
King's Heath
BIRMINGHAM
BS14 6SE

Rubble Blues

Before the song begins, Nehemiah takes up a position just off centre stage, with a butler's cloth draped over his left arm.

CHORUS	ACTIONS
Verse one	
a)	
It was the month of Kislev	*N mimes pouring wine and*
In the twentieth year	*tasting it until he is*
That Artaxerxes	*interrupted by his brother*
Was king around here	
When Hanani my brother	*Enter H and friends. N and H*
came from Judah	*warmly greet each other*
With some men	

To tell me all about Jerusalem

H talks to N

b)
He said that folks back home
Were living kinda rough

H points in direction of Jerusalem
H and "men" scratch heads and
under arms, and turn out their

Times were kinda hard

pockets. H and "men" knock on
their heads with their knuckles

And the neighbours kinda
tough
Well I sat down and wept, 'cos

H and "men" put up fists. N
getting sadder and more
depressed. N kneels on one knee,
and starts weeping

The next thing I heard
The walls were broken down
and the
Gates all burned

H puts hand on N's shoulder. N
looks up at H. H tells the final bit
of bad news.

Chorus
I got the rubble blues

N drops down onto both knees
and sobs into his cloth. All start

I got the rubble blues
When I heard the news
I got the rubble blues

swaying in time with the music
N looks out at audience
N returns to weeping. Exit H
and friends

Verse two
a)
So for several days I mourned

N attempts to eat something,
goes off the idea, and turns to
prayer

And I fasted

N looks up to heaven arms
outstretched to sides

I prayed to God
"You gotta do something
drastic.
I confess OK we acted wickedly,
But please give me success
today."

Spoken rather loudly by N

N hangs head in shame

N gets up with new
determination

b)
I'd a job at the palace, cup
bearer to the King

N puts butler's cloth over left
arm, picks up jug of wine.
Meanwhile enter King and
courtiers

And one day four months later

N's determination fizzles out

103

As I took some wine to him
He said "Nehemiah why you
looking so sad

Surely working for me can't be
all that bad"

Chorus

I got the rubble blues, Your
Majesty
I got the rubble blues, Your
Majesty
Well he was not amused
I got the rubble blues

Verse three
a)
Then he asked me what I
wanted
So I asked him if I could
Go rebuild the city where my
ancestors had stood
I told him how long I'd be gone
And when I would be back

And 'cos God was with me I got
all that I asked

b)
So I jumped on my donkey and
off I went

*(slight pause in the music to
emphasize that there was not an
immediate answer to prayer). N
looks sad as he shuffles sideways
across stage towards the King
N pours wine into cup held by K.
The King sings this bit
N looks sad and turns away from
King*

*N faces K, who is swaying
slightly to the music with his
courtiers*

K shows disapproval

*K turns to N. N looks surprised.
N hastily clasps hands and looks
up
N moves across stage to King
N points in direction of Jerusalem
then points at ground
N looks at watch*

*N holds out hands towards K in
gesture of "that's all".
King shakes N's hand, N looks
surprised and backs away, hands
still outstretched
Others form up behind N in a line
centre stage, and start marching
in time to the music. N looks at
army, then at audience with
delight. N joins in*

*One of the "others" gets down on
all fours as the donkey and N
jumps on his back. Donkey starts*

Took my letter to the West
Euphrates Government
But when Sanballat and Tobiah
heard why I'd been sent

walking on the spot in time with
music and army.
N and the donkey continue same
movements
Enter S and T, noses in the air,
looking indignant. N gives them
the scrolls

Those provincial officials were
so highly indignant

S and T move across stage
sniffing indignantly at N.

Chorus

They got those rubble blues
They got those rubble blues

All sway in time to the music
S and T exit. N and donkey pull
faces after them.

When they heard my news

(strum a few extra bars of A if
necessary to give S and T time to
exit)

They got those rubble blues

Verse four
a)
Well me and my donkey and all
the king's men eventually
arrived in Jerusalem
But for the first three days I
didn't tell anyone

All continue to move on the spot

N looks around sadly
N puts finger to his lips and says
"shh"
N looks about furtively, glancing
over shoulder, etc. Army

Why I'd come or that I had gone
b)
Out one night really late with
some mates
Rode my donkey and inspected
the walls and the gates
But there was so much rubble all
around The King's Pool
That my poor old donkey just
couldn't get through

become's N's mates
N beckons to the others who join
him
All look about at the gates, etc.
Donkey stops suddenly and jerks
N who gets off and tries pushing
and pulling. Donkey flatly
refuses. Others join in, without
success
All push and pull the donkey in
time with the music

Chorus

He'd got the rubble blues,

Ee-yaw
He'd got the rubble blues,
Ee-yaw
Rubble in his hooves
He got the rubble blues

*Donkey lifts up one "hoof" and
points at it with the other "hoof"*

*N and mates say "aah"
Mates become priests and
leaders, etc.*

Verse five

a)
"So I called the priests and the
leaders
And my fellow Jews
I said "It's time you

*This piece should be spoken, up
till "new gates". Play single
chords where indicated
N calls the others around him and
wags his finger at them*

Faced up to a few home truths
Our city's a ruin,
Our name a disgrace

*N points at the ruins about
N hangs his head, hand on his
heart*

Till we rebuild the walls and put
up some new gates"

*N looks up, raises his arms, and
mimes opening gates*

b)
Then I told them how my work
had been inspired by God

They said "Let's rise up and
build" and got ready to start

*N gets down on his knees
Others gather round N and pull
him up onto his feet with a big
jump, saying "Let's rise up and
build!" N looks pleased as the
others get into a line facing the
audience and start to work*

"The God of heaven will give us
success
We're his servants let's clear up
this mess

*Sung by everyone or by two
individuals*

Chorus

*All mime digging in time with
the music*

Let's get this rubble moved

We'll get this rubble moved
And the bricks all hewed
Let's get this rubble moved"

*One person mimes chiseling at
the wall
Continued digging, and
shovelling*

Verse six
a)
Then Sanballat and Tobiah and
an arab named Geshem
Started making fun of us in
front of their friends
They said "A wall made of rubble
won't be very sound

"Why, even a fox could knock it
down"
b)
But their laughter stopped as we
filled in the gaps

Enter S, T, and G

(Key returns to A)
*Others walk around the wall
pointing, looking down their
noses, and laughing*
*Spoken together or
individually*
*One of the others pokes a finger at
the wall and all laugh hilariously
after "knock it down"*
*They stop laughing as the
builders leap into action . . .*
*Music continues playing for a
few bars while actors form a line
each miming that they are
holding swords in one hand. The
men "number" from left to right.
No. 1 with trowel lays cement
with a "shler" noise. No. 2 places
brick; "squelch" noise. The others
do the same thing. It is done in
time with the music.*

S, T, and G huddle together

They started making plots to get us
killed in attacks

Builders mime quick prayers

So we prayed to God and being
warned of their plans

*Builders hold swords in one
hand, and build with the other*

We carried on building with
swords in our hands
b)
I told the people "Don't worry
God's with us stay calm

*N turns to face the people who are
still holding their swords, but
their knees are shaking*
Enter bugler
*N indicates in a wide circle the
wall shading his eyes with his
hand*

My bugler's ready to sound the
alarm.
Because the work is spread out all
over the wall

Gather round me
when you hear him call

N beckons to others who bunch around

S, T, and G creep up to the wall as if to attack

Chorus

(Tune only, chorus imitating trumpet, or by instruments)

Builders spot attackers and gather round N, presenting a united front. S, T, and G retreat and exit, and all cheer

Verse seven
a)
On the 25th day of the month of Elul

N looking visibly tired but happy, stands centre stage. The others gather behind him, smiling

Having cleared away hundreds of tons of ru-bull

No 1 holds up 10 fingers
No 2 holds up 5 fingers
No 3 holds up 10 (equalling 25)

The wall had been finished in just 52 days

Builders mime pushing aside rubble

Our enemies realized that they had lost face

S, T, and G slink across stage and avoid looking at the finished wall. They raise fists at the builders

b)
They knew that with God's help they had suffered defeat

N turns and smiles triumphantly at the others. All raise their arms and praise God. S, T, and G cower and exit.

And just to make their humiliation complete
All our Jewish exiles returned to the homeland
While the members of the sacred Temple choir sang

Some builders become exiles. They all welcome each other N becomes like a conductor and ushers the others into a line in front of him. Tallest at the back, they hold their hands against their chest as a choir and hum different notes until they are in tune with the guitar.

Chorus

Goodbye you rubble blues

Goodbye you rubble blues

Hello fellow Jews
Goodbye you rubble blues
Goodbye you rubble blues
Goodbye you rubble blues
Hello fellow Jews
Goodbye you rubble blues

They sing the chorus through for the first time in mock falsetto voices. They sing as N conducts. They sing it for the second time properly and N joins them in the line and they sway from side to side waving their hands.

Endpeace *by Ronni Lamont*

Introduction

This very simple piece is a retelling of the well-known Passion story in a fresh and moving way (no pun intended!)

It works with people of all ages and differing abilities and is, in many ways, an ideal piece to help a sketch-orientated group to break out into something different.

This version of *Endpeace* is a much-refined workshop piece. It has proved very popular, mainly, we think, because it helps the participants and audience work through the emotions of the Passion.

Bible basis

■ The piece uses elements from all Gospel accounts of the Passion.

Production notes

Endpeace has been developed to work with two specific music tracks, *Heart's Desire* and *Endpeace* from *The Single Factor* album by Camel. (The two tracks run into each other). Of course, there is nothing to stop you using ideas from this presentation with another piece of music, but you will have to adapt these music-specific notes if you do.

Useful exercises

What we give you here is the basic floor pattern and time sequence of the piece, using the words of the song where possible. It is up to you to make it work as a piece well before you start rehearsing (see the *Making moves* framework) and the group need to know their individual strengths and weaknesses. We speak from experience – we once cast someone as Jesus who moved as if they had two arms in plaster and was trying to direct traffic! You might also find some still images work useful, such as *Tell a story* and *Instant pictures* (feelings).

The piece is adaptable in the number of people used, depending on the capabilities of your group, but remember that you need enough disciples to physically carry Jesus.

Characters

- Jesus
- Judas
- Soldiers
- Disciples
- All characters can be female or male.

Endpeace

- At the start the stage is set as below:

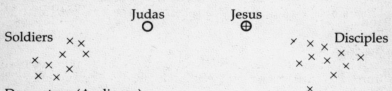

Downstage (Audience)

- All face the back of the acting area.

Cues

- The music begins, "The light is fading, the course invading . . . " On the word "course" Jesus turns round and slowly moves to centre stage. This is his prayer alone. Simple clean movements, indicating pleading to heaven, reaching out to the disciples and into himself.
- By "And you must go" (the first one) Jesus kneels and is still.

110

During the above, the disciples are also moving. Exact timing of this will be a factor of your working space and the moves that your group devise. A simple and effective pattern is: As Jesus reaches the centre the disciples move to centre stage left and stand in an inward-facing circle. They place their arms on each other's shoulders, sway to the left, then right, then freeze as if asleep but standing up.

■ "And you must go" (still the first one). We now introduce Judas to the scene. Again the style is simple and clear. Judas turns and approaches Jesus from behind. Jesus rises and Judas approaches. The two look at each other – think of what this look is saying and experiment. Avoid the temptation to "make faces". Let the drama come out of the simple movements and the audience's knowledge of the situation. After a pause, Judas places his hands on Jesus' shoulders and kisses him on the cheek. Judas stands back as the soldiers turn and approach Jesus. You need to work out a way for this to happen – it should be smooth and militaristic. When we did this workshop piece in East Germany, the soldiers goose-stepped!

■ The soldiers surround Jesus, turn, and march off with Jesus in the midst. Practise this until it works. You are looking for a contrast between Jesus the Man of Peace and the unthinking militarism of the soldiers.

■ "And you must go" (second time). Reduce the music volume and have someone read: "It was nine o'clock in the morning when they crucified him" – or make a tape with the reading on it. Fade the music back up. The rest of the music is instrumental, and at workshops people manage to fit the actions to the music, but it is more important than ever here that the director knows the music well.

The idea of this section is that the crucifixion is taking place in front of the acting area – where the audience is. The audience will have the reactions of the various characters to tell it what is going on, but, again, avoid over-reacting with the face.

■ Judas enters and stands downstage centre. His feelings are confused – remorse, anger, pity. He focuses on "the cross" and so sets in the minds of the audience where it is to be found.

■ The disciples enter next. This is always one of our favourite parts at a workshop because they nearly always seem to find a good, natural grouping. They are a tightly-formed group, supportive and protective towards each other. They focus on the same point as Judas.

■ The soldiers march on and form a barrier across the front of the stage. They are on duty and you will need to find stances that reflect this. At this stage, the layout is as below;

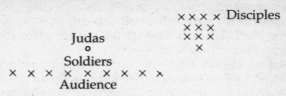

- Narrator reads: "With a loud cry, Jesus died".
- The stage positions change rapidly – Jesus is dead and everything is different. The soldiers relax – they turn and sit/ stand in small groups miming "off-duty" activities in a fairly low-key manner; sleeping, drinking, etc.
- The disciples move across the area to upstage right.
- Judas turns and exits upstage left.
- The next section calls for clever stage management, espcially if you are using an area with an off-stage that is not screened from the audience. The disciples must pick up the "dead" Jesus and carry him on. One person can do this in a fireman's lift, or the whole group can surround Jesus to lift him, (made easier if Jesus is lying on chairs). It will work without a screen, but is much better if you don't show the works.
- The disciples carry the body to centre stage and put it down. They then sit or kneel around Jesus, facing outwards and downwards. They are lost and uncertain what to do now.
- Now the big moment as Jesus returns to life. Try to imagine the first heart-beat, the gaining of strength, and the clearing of consciousness, then translate this into movement. Jesus starts to rise; use body tension to spread the movement, until he stands to face the disciples. You will have to work on this; too many interpretations of this section look a bit like synchronised swimming done by a solo swimmer. Think strong all the time.
- The other people on stage see and hear nothing of this until Jesus bends and touches one of the disciples. All the disciples turn and look. What would you feel like if it happened to you? Fear? Amazement? Relief? Encourage each disciple to work on their reaction but, whatever they feel, they follow Jesus as he leads them upstage. The group freeze as they reach the back of the stage, as if a photographer had caught them walking off.
- In the music there should now be a ten-beat pause before the

last guitar note. You now see the importance of someone knowing the music really well and working out the floor pattern and basic moves in advance! Use these directions and the music to be really sure of what you're doing when you come to rehearse the piece. Use this note for the guards to turn around suddenly and stare at the empty space.

■ One by one the guards exit to their original positions, walking around the space previously occupied by Jesus, reacting differently to it; disbelief, cynicism, uncertainty, etc.

■ As the music is finally fading out, Judas enters and looks at the space. You will need to work on what he is feeling and thinking at this point. We find that, in practice, if you've worked through the piece, Judas' reaction comes quite naturally to the person playing the part. He raises his head to look at the audience, then slowly walks off.

■ The music fades to leave an empty stage, apart from the still image of Jesus and the disciples.

That's the end of the piece as we've developed it for workshops, but do feel free to experiment with the end to make it work for your group, audience and, of course, the geography of your performace space.

Bibliography

Practical/general

Using the Bible in Drama	J and S Stickley	Bible Society
100+ Ideas for Drama (games & activities)	Scher and Verral	Heinemann Educational
Another 100+ Ideas for Drama	Scher and Verral	Heinemann Educational
Theatrecraft	N Forde	Marc Europe
Steps of Faith	G and J Stevenson	Kingsway

Practical/sketches

Time to Act	P Burbridge and M Watts	Hodder and Stoughton
Lightning Sketches	P Burbridge and M Watts	Hodder and Stoughton
Laughter in Heaven	M Watts (ed)	Marc Europe
Red Letter Days	P Burbridge and M Watts	Hodder and Stoughton
Scene One	Martin, Kelso, & others	Kingsway
Footnotes	S and J Stickley	Hodder and Stoughton
Drama Recipe Book	A McDonald and S Stickley	Monarch
One Stage Further	N Forde	Marc Europe
Back to Back's Little Black Paperback Book	F Grace	Kingsway
Playing with Fire (5 full-length stage plays)	P Burbridge (ed)	Marc Europe

Other creative resources from Bible Society

Picture It!
by Paul Clowney

Packed full of ideas on how you can use your artistic skills and interests to serve God and his church. Written by artist, designer, and teacher Paul Clowney, specifically to help encourage a wider use of the visual arts in the Church.

Using the Bible in Drama
by Steve and Janet Stickley and Jim Belben

Now established as a standard work on the subject of starting a church drama group. It presents for free performance some of Footprints Theatre Company's most famous sketches, and also includes advice on warming up, studying the Bible, writing through improvisation, performing, and presenting your sketches.

Show Me!
by Judy Gattis Smith

Fifteen techniques – and thirty ready-to-use examples – revealing how to use drama with children aged 3-13. Written by a Director of Christian Education in a church in Williamsburg, Virginia, USA, then tested, revised, and republished for use in the UK.

Everyone's a Winner
by Jim Belben and Trevor Cooper

The fruit of eight years extensive exploration on how games can be used to explore the Bible. It contains thirteen practical, thoroughly-tested games, role-plays, and simulations to explore the Bible. Some of the subjects covered are: boy-girl relationships, money, Old Testament relationship to New Testament, how we got our Bible, what should the church be doing, how do we make decisions, and much much more.